MODULAR
HOUSE
DESIGN

MODULAR HOUSE DESIGN

The Key to Complete Construction Efficiency

Frederick Uhlen Hop

PRENTICE HALL, Englewood Cliffs, New Jersey 07632

Library of Congress Cataloging-in-Publication Data

Hop, Frederick Uhlen.
    Modular house design : the key to complete construction efficiency
    Frederick Uhlen Hop.
        p.   cm.
    Includes index.
    ISBN 0-13-599424-1
    1. Modular coordination (Architecture)   2. House construction.
    I. Title.
    TH860.H67 1988
    728.3'7--dc19   87-24170
                                                                   CIP

Editorial/production supervision and
    interior design: *Carol Atkins*
Cover design: *Wanda Lubelska*
Manufacturing buyer: *Peter Havens*

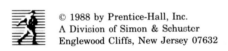

© 1988 by Prentice-Hall, Inc.
A Division of Simon & Schuster
Englewood Cliffs, New Jersey 07632

Printed in the United States of America
10 9 8 7 6 5 4 3 2 1

ISBN 0-13-599424-1

Prentice-Hall International (UK) Limited, *London*
Prentice-Hall of Australia Pty. Limited, *Sydney*
Prentice-Hall Canada Inc., *Toronto*
Prentice-Hall Hispanoamericana, S.A., *Mexico*
Prentice-Hall of India Private Limited, *New Delhi*
Prentice-Hall of Japan, Inc., *Tokyo*
Simon & Schuster Asia Pte. Ltd., *Singapore*
Editora Prentice-Hall do Brasil, Ltda., *Rio de Janeiro*

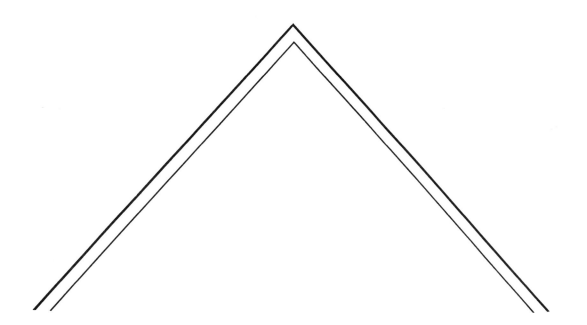

Contents

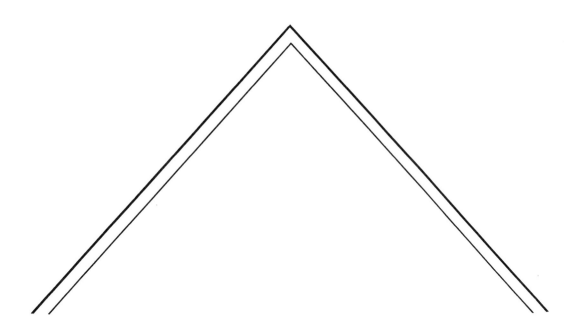

Preface

Modular design is a key factor to economy and efficiency in modern house construction. In this book, the reference to modular design encompasses all methods of building whether a house is stick built on site or fabricated on an assembly line. Adhering to modular design simplifies the assembly process. Most of the building materials on the market today are modular in one or more dimensions. The greatest saving of labor and material will be realized by using a house plan that requires the least measuring, cutting, and customizing of individual pieces. For the carpenter, a modular plan is a joy to work with, as it substantially reduces computation and increases assembly speed.

Keys to the modular system are discussed throughout this book. Part I provides the information needed to understand the uniqueness of various material sizes and explains how they fit together with coordinate components. All the key modular dimensions are learned. The reader will emerge equipped to accurately assess those dimensions which are fully modular, those which are partially modular, and those where modularity has been substantially ignored or accidentally hit upon in a few isolated places.

Part II equips the reader to systematically design and draw a plan that is structurally modular from the foundation to a completed structure. A simplified dimensioning system, one which is more logical, is presented. The reader will also learn to recognize nonmodular plans at a glance and be able to modify them to modular dimensions.

Part III carefully details stairway design and construction. Why should we have a chapter about stairs in a book about modularity? Stairs are designed to fit pre-determined wells, or the wells are designed to accomodate predesigned stairs. The modularity concept applies to stairs because the primary design objective is to show a set of assembled stairs, each of which is identical in height and depth (rise and run). In a sense, the builder, via a proper design, will construct a stairway with custom modularized steps. Part III provides the know-how for designing, laying out, and assembling such a staircase. Hypotenuse tables (first in print), found in the Appendix, will aid in the laying out of the stringers.

Mastery of this book will be an exciting venture into relms of construction and design that have hitherto been unexplained or vaguely alluded to. On the practical side, there is much money and effort to be saved when the concepts herein are put into practice by either a novice or a full-time builder. Good luck, whatever your project or objective.

Frederick Uhlen Hop

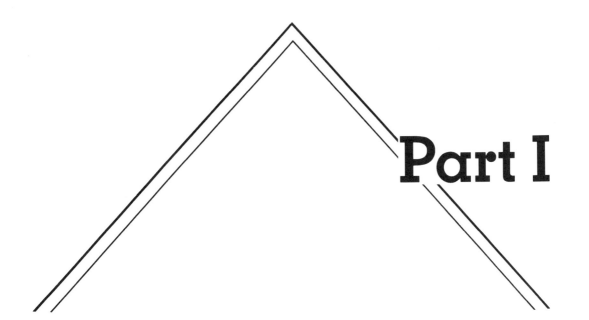

Part I

Characteristics
of
Modularity

1 Modular Design

The words modulus, module, modular, and modularity are used to mean several different things in the construction industry. *Module* means a standardized component. *Modular design* refers to a coordinated system that makes use of standardized material units without waste. *Modulus* refers to the size of the unit. The term *modularity* is used herein to denote a concept of design that features maximum construction efficiency and minimum material waste through the use of modular components.

There are other related uses of these terms. In the plumbing industry, the one-piece, fiberglass, combination tub and shower is called a "module." The plywood companies some years ago designed a straight-line floor frame assembly that accepts full sheets of plywood. It was labeled a "modular system of joist spacing." When factories began to fabricate parts of homes, the assembly lines made modular units that would fit together on the site. These were called "panelized" or "modular" homes. Early publications by the National Forest Products Association called this system the "unicom" method.

2 Designer's Objective

Whatever these various meanings, there is one common objective for the designer: to draw a structural plan that makes use of modular materials with little or no cutting. Unfortunately for the builder, not many architect-drawn plans are available that emphasize modularity. The typical architectural emphasis is likely to focus on aesthetic features, the beauty of a design. It then falls to the builder to try to adapt the existing material modules to an uncoordinated plan.

3 Text Objective

An objective of this text is to show how a plan can be modular as well as attractive. It is usually possible to coordinate a pleasing appearance with economically structured design. The reader will learn the significant and telltale dimensions that denote a plan that considers modularity. With some study and a little practice, the serious reader will be able to assess the superior plan, the plan that requires the least amount of revision. By applying this knowledge, thousands of dollars can be saved on a single house project.

4 Basic Modulus Materials

Production of two material units has enabled the concept of modular construction to become a reality. One of these was the development of the precast concrete block; the other was the lamination technique that gave us the plywood sheet (Fig. 1).

When builders realized the coordination potential between these two modules and others like them, the industry began a significant change in construction technique. Both of the materials were standardized on the 4″ modular cube. Roughly speaking, all coordinating modular materials to follow are based on division by four. For example, the width of plywood (4′) coordinates with the length of three laid blocks (16″ modules × 3 = 4′); plywood in lengthwise position (8′) coordinates with 6 blocks

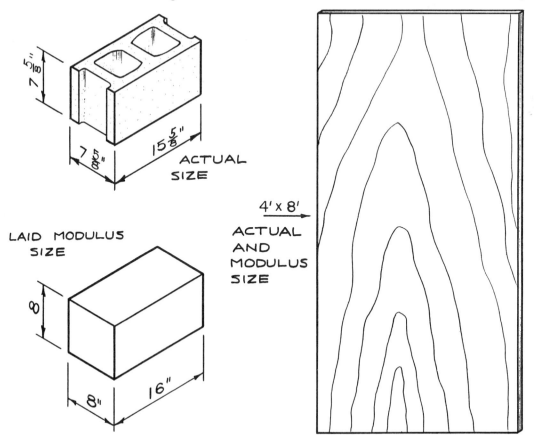

Figure 1 The concrete block and the plywood sheet are standardized units which form the basis of modularity in the United States.

(Fig. 2). The most common standardized block is the stretcher. It measures 16″ long, which includes the mortar joint when laid in a course. The height and most common depth of the basic block are both 8″ laid in a wall.

5 Material-Coordinating Formula

With this simple bit of coordinating knowledge, the designer has a mathematical tool at his disposal. It will be referred to as the 3-for-4 theorem. The applications are many. There are 3 concrete block units for every 4 running feet (linear horizontal distance). Knowing this, we can accurately assess the length of a block foundation simply by counting the blocks. More significantly, the designer will recognize the specific linear dimensions that accept full blocks without remainders. For every 3 blocks, there are 4' of length. To find the feet when a quantity of block units is known, *divide* the quantity by 3 and *multiply* the result by 4.

Formula: (Units ÷ 3) × 4' = length
Sample problem: 36 units ÷ 3 = 12 × 4' = 48'

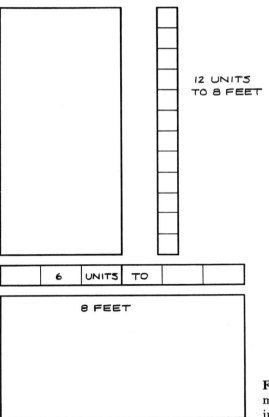

Figure 2 Blocks and plywood moduli coordinate to form a spacing system.

6 Recognizing Modular Dimensions

To determine whether a dimension fits the unit modulus, simply multiply the dimension by ¾. When the result is a full number, it means that the dimension is evenly divisible by 16″ (the block length modulus). It will accommodate full block units. There will be no fractional joist and stud spacing at one end of the house left over, as would be the case with a nonmodular dimension, since these wood parts are usually spaced on the 16″ modulus. The following are problems using sample dimensions that are modular.

$$\text{¾} \times 60' = 45 \text{ units}$$
$$\text{¾} \times 48' = 36 \text{ units}$$
$$\text{¾} \times 41'\text{-}4'' = 31 \text{ units}$$
$$\text{¾} \times 42'\text{-}8'' = 32 \text{ units}$$

COMPUTATION BY CALCULATOR

When a dimension ends with inches, the feet and inches should be converted to inches before dividing. By so doing, the result will be in full numbers when the dimension proves to be modular. An inexpensive calculator operates with decimals. The moduli for blocks and frame spacing are 4″ (⅓ of a foot) and 8″ (⅔ of a foot). These inches are the excess beyond the foot length of one block (1′-4″) and two blocks (2′-8″). Neither ⅓ nor ⅔ can be multiplied on a calculator with complete accuracy. Take the following example using the dimension forty-one feet, four inches of foundation length (41′-4″). Three for four is three-quarters or 75 one-hundredths.

$$.75 \times 41.333333 = 30.999999$$

We know that ¾ of 41'-4" is actually 31 full units of 16" spaces. It can be arrived at mentally with ease by going to the root number (the closest 4' module) and adding the additional single unit. Forty feet is the closest root number divisible by 4. Forty feet times three-quarters nets 30 units plus the one additional unit gives 31 units. If the dimension is 42'-8", we could go to the 44 root module and subtract one unit, or we could use the 40' module and add two units. To use the calculator with complete accuracy, let us transpose the sample dimension of 41'-4" into inches first. Next divide by the 16" unit modulus. Set up for calculator or long hand, the problem looks like this:

$$41' \times 12" = 492" + 4" = 496" \div 16" = 31 \text{ units}$$

Note that this comes out exactly even, as it should when the dimension is modular.

Let us take an example *that is not modular* in any sense.

$$¾ \times 45'\text{-}10" = ?$$

Setting up the problem, we have

$$45' \times 12" = 540" + 10" = 550" \div 16" = 34.375 \text{ units}$$

NONMODULAR FIGURES

Feet that are trailed by the following inches are never modular for the application of plywood or concrete blocks: 1, 2, 3, 5, 6, 7, 9, 10, and 11. These figures will always produce an odd-sized space in the framing structures (floors, walls, ceilings, and rafters). In the foundation, they will require cutting or breaking of blocks. The only inch figures following feet that are modular are 4 and 8. It will also be found, a little further on in this study, that the 4" figure is modular only when preceded by an odd-numbered foot and the 8" figure when preceded by an even-numbered foot. 41'-4" is modular. 42'-8" is modular. 41'-8" and 42'-4" are nonmodular.

7 Modular Materials

Many synthetic materials have been coordinated to make the modularity principle possible. A common brick lays up six to a block face (some newer magnum sizes do not modularize with blocks in length, but can be made to coordinate at certain course levels). There are many sheet materials that modularize with blocks. These are fiberboard (Celotex), hard board (Masonite), Styrofoam, gypsum wall board, particle board, and all the types of plywood and paneling. Their common modulus is 4′ × 8′. Common ceiling tile sizes are 12″ × 12″, 16″ × 16″, and 24″ × 48″. The odd nonmodular 9″ × 9″ floor tile has been phased out in favor of the current modular 12″ × 12″ units. One of the few remaining nonmodular areas in construction is the bathroom, with its 5′ tub and 4¼″ tiles.

8 Modular Plan Dimensions

There are key plan dimensions that the designer should memorize. The memorization should be of the graphic, visual type. The person should see in his or her mind's eye a visual image of the material and be immediately able to associate the size to the image. This is not a monumental assignment. It is like the games we had as children: the Lincoln logs, the erector sets, and more recently, the snap-together plastic toys.

VISUALIZING UNIT COORDINATES

Visualize the stretcher block. It is 8″ high and 16″ long. Now visualize a sheet of plywood standing vertically on top of three blocks lying end to end (Fig. 3). Three 16″ blocks measure 48″ end to end, which is the same as the width of the plywood. Now

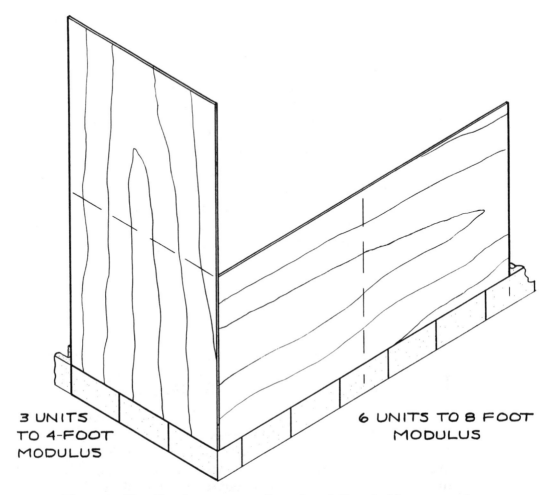

**3 UNITS
TO 4-FOOT
MODULUS**

**6 UNITS TO 8 FOOT
MODULUS**

Figure 3　Visualize the concrete and wood moduli as double squares when sketching in addition to the 3-for-4 concept.

lay the plywood down on edge horizontally. Picture six blocks under it. Six units of 16″ equal the 96″ length of the plysheet. When visualizing these two materials, you should also think in proportionate sizes. Both the block and the plywood are twice as long as they are wide. Focus mentally on two squares comprising the rectangle. This visualizing helps greatly to maintain correct proportions when sketching details of construction.

CHARACTERISTICS OF STRUCTURAL MEMBERS

The next step in this exercise is to consider the manner in which the modular materials fit onto or are attached to the structural members. Structural members, such as floor joists, wall studs, and roof rafters, have standard girth dimensions. Girth means the cross-section thickness and width (the distance around). These sizes will vary only slightly due to the effects of moisture or dryness, which cause them to swell or shrink. Girth has little relation to modular planning. Length and spacing of structural members have a direct influence on modular coordination. All the larger members (2 × 6 through 2 × 12) come in even lengths starting with 8′ and ending with 24′. This structural lumber is referred to as *dimension lumber*. There is one modular exception in the dimension lumber category. This is the precut stud. "Precuts," as they are nicknamed, come precisely cut to identical lengths of 92⅝″. The length has been established as a universally coordinated module to fit interior wall-covering modules of drywall and paneling. It coordinates with a single sole plate and a double top plate to form the required height.

FOUR-FOOT MODULUS

The most significant dimensions that are first encountered in designing or assessing a plan will be the exterior overall dimensions. When a block is the unit modulus of the foundation and will be coordinated with modular sheathing above, the most economical dimensional sizes will be those that are divisible by 4′. Foundation rectangles of the following overall dimensions are examples of perfect modules: 24 × 40, 28 × 52, and 28′ × 60′. Wings or ells off a rectangle will coordinate perfectly when they follow the same rule. These major modules (divisible by 4) create the potential for little or no waste throughout the floor, the exterior walls, and the ceiling joists. Any departure from this size formula automatically raises the cost of the house by causing waste through leftover materials. The same modular principle

applies to poured concrete foundations that will have wood
framed structures upon them. Although the fluid concrete has no
modular character, all the materials that go on a poured foundation do.

SPLIT MODULUS

The next significant module may be called the split modulus, or
"mod" for short. It incorporates dimensions that are divisible by
2'. There are unique characteristics of the split mod to visualize
and understand. A foundation of 26 × 40' will accommodate an
even number of block units even though the 26' is divisible by
neither 16" nor 4'. On one of the 40' sides there will be 30 blocks;
on each of the split-mod 26' ends, there will be 19 blocks; on the
back side there will be 29 blocks (Fig. 4). No blocks will need
cutting. This factor occurs because of the 8" depth of the block,
which carries around the corner to fill the half-unit module (26'
÷ 16" = 19½ units). Since blocks are laid in a staggered course
pattern in foundations, the next course will have 30 blocks on
the back side of the foundation and 29 on the front. The split mod
can be correlated with blocks as illustrated. The split-mod dimension does not correlate with stud spacing of 16". There will
always be a half-space (8") module left over with dimensions that
are divisible by 2 but not divisible by 4. This is a minor factor as
it only involves the addition of one stud per wall. The split mod
remains modular with sheathing and siding modules that are
installed vertically. A sheet is cut in half. The cut-off half fills
out the opposite side or end of the house. For example, 26' ends of
a house frame will each take 6½ sheets, or 13 full sheets in all.

SIXTEEN-INCH MODULUS

The third choice of desirable exterior dimensions is any multiple
of feet that can be divided equally by 16" (1¼'). Examples of
these house dimensions are 25'-4" × 38'-8" or 26'-8" × 45'-4".
These figures, although common in their divisibility by 16", pose
completely different considerations for coordination in a wood
structure, which are explained in paragraphs to follow.

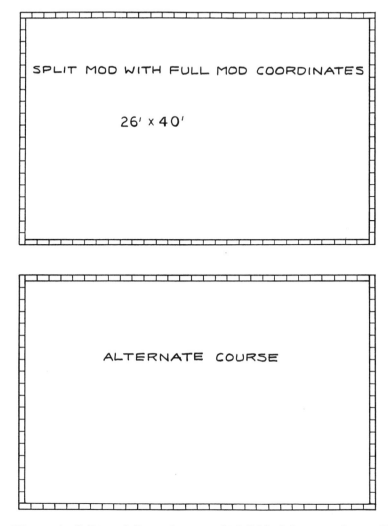

Figure 4   Split mod dimensions can fit full block layouts when well planned.

9 Common Spacing Modulus

Floor joists and wall studs are most commonly spaced 16″ apart. Three spaces form the major modulus similar to the concrete block coordinates. On four wall studs, which make up three spaces, visually place a vertical sheet of plywood (Fig. 5). Now

COORDINATED
FOUNDATION, FRAMEWORK, AND SHEATHING

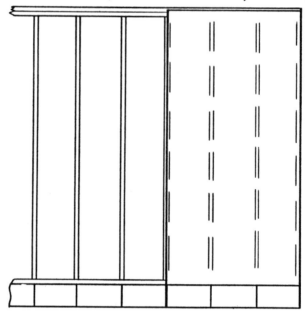

Figure 5   Visualize the coordination of blocks with standard sheets and both sheets and blocks with stud spacing. Stud quantity (16″ OC) will be 3-for-4 plus 1 to close the end of the wall.

associate horizontal major mod dimensions with the plywood and begin to lengthen the wall. A pattern begins to emerge of full units fitting neatly together. See two sheets, then three, then four sheets in place. Mentally note, "four sheets equal 16′—four modules of triple blocks equal 12 blocks—behind the plywood, 12 stud spaces net 13 studs." Add another sheathing module and recompute. This visualizing technique turns the mind into an effective computer of materials and dimensions. Continue the exercise by adding units of plywood. The significant major module dimensions are now clear (Fig. 6). Our early training in arithmetic probably left us with the common skill of counting by twos, either odd or even. Now we are developing the design skill of counting by fours.

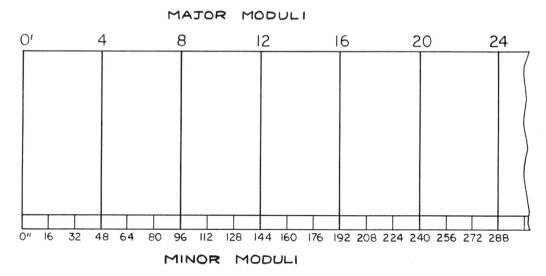

Figure 6 Think major and minor modules when designing. This will contribute to a plan which will save significant material and labor cost.

10 Effect of 16″ Spacing on Wall Length

Consider the effect of adding a single or double 16″ unit of linear space to the full 4′ modules. A house dimension of 40′ will accept 10 full, uncut sheets of sheathing placed vertically on the wall (discounting window and door openings at this point). Add one 16″ minor module of length and space. Now there is an odd space left over at one end of the wall. A vertical third of a sheathing sheet is required to cover this space. Another third will be used on the opposite wall. A third of a sheet is left over.

11 Effect of 16″ Spacing on Floor Design

In the example of a plan length of 41′-4″ (ten major mods plus one minor mod), the floor sheathing will also be affected. Floor sheathing is placed with the long direction running across the

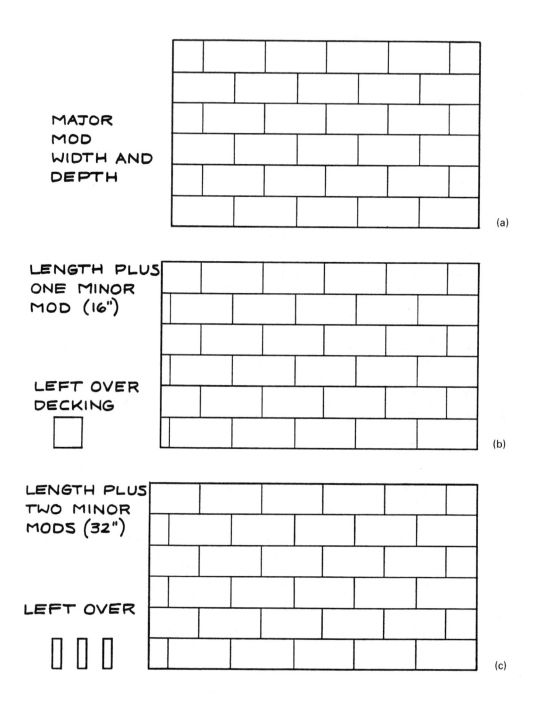

MAJOR
MOD
WIDTH AND
DEPTH

(a)

LENGTH PLUS
ONE MINOR
MOD (16")

LEFT OVER
DECKING

(b)

LENGTH PLUS
TWO MINOR
MODS (32")

LEFT OVER

(c)

Figure 7 A major mod floor deck; a major plus one minor mod floor deck; a major plus two minor mods.

joists. The plywood length being 8', a 40' floor will accept five full sheets per course (Fig. 7a). A 41'-4" floor will require an additional one-sixth of the length of a sheet (Fig. 7b). Additional labor time is required for the cutting that is necessary on every course. The 40' floor (or any dimension divisible by 8) will require sheet cutting (in half) only every other course because the end joints are staggered. The first, third, fifth, and so on, courses will accommodate full sheets. The second and fourth and sixth courses will take the two halves that were cut with one pass of the saw and used to start and end the course. The same characteristic exists with linear frontal dimensions that have two additional 16" moduli added to the basic fours (Fig. 7c). Use the 40' basic four as an example again and add two units of 16". This makes 42'-8". This dimension is now two units beyond the major module of 40' and one unit short of the next module of 44'.

12 Modularity Patterns in Dimensions

By visualizing actual figures in modular dimensions, a consistent pattern emerges. The skill of recognizing this pattern makes it possible to evaluate the effects of specific dimensions on labor time and material use. Assume that, after sufficient practice, the major 4' moduli from 4' to 100' can be readily recognized. For each 16' minor module added to a major module, 1'-4" will be added. The foot number is always odd. The inch number is always 4. When two minor moduli units of 16" (32") are added, it is discovered that the inch figure is always 8 and the preceding foot number is always even. Therefore, the single minor unit extension with an odd number plus 4" and double unit addition with an even number plus 8" emerges as a recognizable pattern. For example, a major module is 40'. That module plus one minor module is 41'-4". The same module (40') plus a double minor module is 42'-8".

The principles to remember are these:

- Odd-numbered feet following a major mod plus 4" comprise major modules of 4' plus one minor module of 16".

- Even-numbered feet following a major mod plus 8" comprise major modules of 4' plus two minor modules of 16" (or the next higher major module minus 16").
- Overall dimensions ending in inches other than 4 or 8 are nonmodular.

Visualizing and memorizing these principles will enable a consumer or builder to recognize whether a plan has been developed with modularity as an objective. Unfortunately, most plans on the market today, available across the counter or through the mail, are not based on modularity. As a designer, you are now in possession of the principles that are needed to revise the exterior overall dimensions of such plans. By so doing, material cost can be saved or additional floor space can be gained at little or no cost. As a final exercise, let us view a series of linear dimensions. To make the characteristics stand out, the major 4' modular figures are circled. For practice, continue the figures on up to 100'.

⟨20⟩-0	21-4	22-8	⟨24⟩-0	25-4	26-8
⟨28⟩-0	29-4	30-8	⟨32⟩-0	33-4	34-8
⟨36⟩-0	37-4	38-8	⟨40⟩-0	41-4	42-8
⟨44⟩-0	45-4	46-8	⟨48⟩-0	49-4	50-8

13 Modularity Considerations with Floor Joists

The most efficient depths (spans) for a wood floor are 12', 16', 20', 24', 28', and 32'. Thirty-two feet is a maximum depth with the use of a pair of single joists end to end across the span. Sixteen feet is the maximum possible span found on most stress tables for a 2 × 12 joist. Fabricated truss joists will be required for spans over 16'. No dimension lumber is readily available above 12 nominal inches. For practical considerations, the house depth of 28' should not be exceeded unless a thorough understanding of the structural loads from above exists. The problem associated with spans of joists between 14 and 16′ long is springiness in the floor. Although the longer and larger joist may carry the weight adequately, the floor may not feel rigid when walking on it.

The next most efficient depth modules are those divisible by 2′ as far as the floor is concerned. The primary consideration is the available lengths of joists and the construction methods to coordinate the joists with plywood sheathing widths. Therefore, the 2′ dimension lumber modulus is our focal design interest when considering the total span.

14 Optional Girder Placement

Girders are beams of steel or built-up wood designed and placed to support the interior ends of joists and bearing partitions. Girders do not have to be centered between foundations as long as the lumber girth of the joists is large enough to meet the span code of the longest joist used. The following are some feasible combinations of floor depths.

20′ depth
Two 10′ joists butted
One 12′ and one 8′ joist butted over a girder

22′ depth
One 10′ and one 12′ joist butted over a girder
Two 12′ joists lapped over a centered girder

24′ depth
Two 12′ joists butted over a centered girder
One 12′ and one 14′ joist lapped over an off-center girder

26′ depth
One 12′ and one 14′ butted over a girder
Two 14′ joists lapped over a centered girder

28′ depth
Two 14′ joists butted over a centered girder
One 14′ and one 16′ joist lapped over an off-center girder

EFFECT ON PLYWOOD SHEATHING

The plywood sheathing modulus to be considered when designing floor depth is 4'. This is because the plywood will be placed with its long direction across the joists (at right angles). Therefore, each course of sheathing is 4' wide. Floor depth dimensions divisible by 4 and floor lengths divisible by 8 will net 100% use of plywood sheets. For example, a floor 24' × 40' will take exactly 30 sheets of plywood. Six courses deep times five sheets long equals 30 units. Full use of plywood can be achieved with the 2' split-mod depths when the length dimensions of the floor are held to figures evenly divisible by 8. An example of this would be a floor size of 26' × 48'. The only additional cost in such a dimension will be the labor required to saw the last course of sheathing lengthwise into 2' widths (three sheets cut into six pieces; Fig. 8).

SPLIT MODULI DEPTH (2')

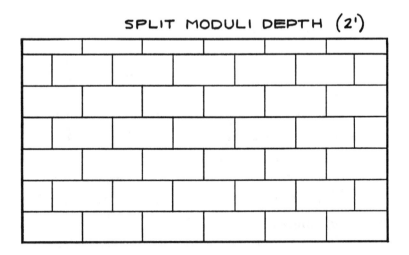

FULL MODULI LENGTH

Figure 8 Split mod depth with full mod length requires ripping of sheets lengthwise.

15 Visualizing Material Quantities

There is a fringe benefit in mastering the technique of visualizing the coordination of materials to dimensions. Figuring out a bill of materials becomes an easy mental exercise. Much of it can be accomplished with minimum mathematics. It is a simple system of counting units instead of computing areas by square feet. For example, the conscientious student will find it quite possible to answer quickly and accurately such questions as: How many sheets of sheathing are needed for the exterior walls of a rectangular house that is 24 × 48′? The visual process kicks into gear and grinds out 6 units on one end, 12 units on a side;

$$6 + 12 = 18 \times 2 = 36 \text{ sheets.}$$

COUNTING DIMENSION LUMBER NEEDS

There is one exception to the counting method. When inventorying for dimension units (joists, studs, and rafters), the problem is one of space and perimeter as contrasted to area coverage. The sheathing unit that covers three 16″ wall spaces will have four studs. Look at the back of your hand with your thumb folded back out of sight. There are three spaces, but four fingers. The 3-for-4 theorem is used by simply adding one lumber unit to close the last space. Visualize two sheets of plywood. There are now six studs plus one for 8′ of coverage (seven studs in all). The 3-for-4 spatial concept can be memorized as a fractional multiplier once the visualizing skill has been learned. Regardless of the total length of a house, there will be three stud space units for each 4′ with the 16″ spacing system. Add one stud to the space count to obtain the quantity of common studs. An additional stud is added for each corner. This 3-for-4 plus one on the end formula will be accurate for partitions with no openings and no intersections. For an intersection add one stud. For a single door add one stud. The one displaced by the usual 32″ rough opening will provide a trimmer for one side, so only one additional stud is required to make the other trimmer. Trimmers are the shortened studs that support the header above. For larger doors, double doors, or wider arches, no extra count need be added, as the displaced studs from the opening will provide both trimmers.

Exterior walls are a different story. The doorways are fairly standardized, with 3′ entry doors the most common and frequently used for front and rear entry. Often there will be a dinette or patio door that displaces enough studs to provide its own trimmers and have one or two left over. The window openings, by virtue of their variable height, are less predictable. Sometimes, displaced partial studs will compensate for the rough sill material that is required below a window.

Two simple methods of estimating a stud count for exterior walls are available. A fairly close estimation will be to compute the perimeter in feet. Count one stud for each linear foot. The second tried and true method is to use the floor plan. Put a little × where each stud is on the plan. Then count the ×s.

16 Modular Partition Intersections

The preceding example assumes the placement of the partition at a point that will utilize one of the studs already in the intersected wall. This will seldom, if ever, happen unless the plan has been specifically designed for it to happen. For it to occur intentionally, the dimensions on the floor plan must place one side or the other of the frame in line with the edge or center of the "on center" stud in the frame it intersects (Fig. 9). When dimensioned to the edge of this stud (the preferred method), a dimension will read in multiples of 16″ plus ¾″ (half the thickness of the stud). Examples are 12′-0¾″, 13′-4¾″, 14′-8¾″, and 16′-0¾″. Each of these examples places the partition on the far side of the on-center stud. A dimension that places the partition on the near side will read in multiples of 16″ minus ¾″. These dimensions will read 11'-11¼", 13'-3¼", 14'-7¼", and 15'-11¼". On the plan, the dimension line arrows must clearly show which side of the frame wall is being aligned to the stud in the frame it intersects. Plans with dimensions to the center of the frame wall indicate a disregard for modular coordination. Such a plan forces the layout carpenter to straddle the location with the wall, thus requiring two extra studs at each intersection (Fig. 10). The other alternative is to move the partition toward the closest stud. This involves a plan revision that may involve major changes. The well-planned modular system makes layout and construction simpler and less costly.

It is possible, and not difficult, to design a house plan with most of the intersections coordinated modularly. The saving in studs and labor is substantial. Floor-plan layout is simpler and more accurate. Parallel placement of walls is made easy because a stud on the opposite wall may be used as a reference point. Wiring and insulating require less time and fitting. The floor frame will also benefit. Since the floor joist is below the stud, the modularly coordinated partition will run alongside the edge of the joist. Where a trimmer joist is specified for partition support, it will be placed on the side of the joist that puts it directly under the partition. This removes the necessity of using cross blocks to support the sheathing. All benefits taken into consideration, the modularly placed partition system is superior.

17 Modular In-Line Framework System

The crowning effort toward a completely modularized framing plan is to assure that all ceiling joists and rafters are coordinated with the walls and floor. Ceiling joists of conventional design will bear directly over common stud positions when placed on the same spacing modules (commonly 16"). In this position, each joist adjacent to a parallel partition provides a nail-backing function for the ceiling skin.

Trusses are usually placed on 24" spacing. With wall studs on 16" centers, every other truss will be positioned directly over the studs that are placed on the major modules divisible by 4' (0',

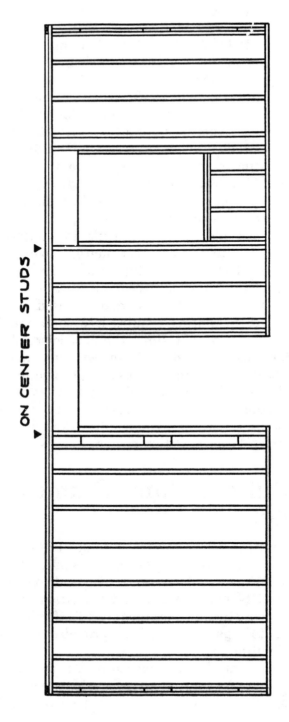

Figure 9 A modularly-planned typical wall saves labor and materials. The stud count averages out to one stud per linear foot.

ON CENTER STUDS

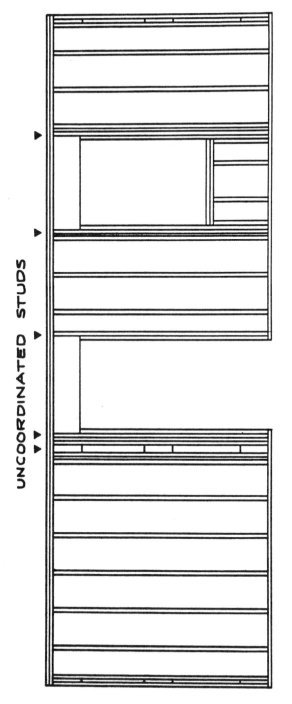

Figure 10 A nonmodular plan disregards material and spacing, causes waste and inefficiency. There will be many more ill-spaced studs to buy and narrow spaces to insulate.

UNCOORDINATED STUDS

4', 8', 12', and so on). Those on 2', 6', 10', 14', and so on, will bear on the double top plate in between the studs. Regardless of whether conventional or trussed, these two arrangements are considered modularly aligned.

18 Conclusions about Modularity

The challenge to the designer who accepts modularity as an objective is to devise a construction plan that will net three results: (1) economical use of materials, (2) efficient use of labor, and (3) a structurally sound and pleasing home. From the foregoing descriptions of the significance of key modular dimensions, some specific and some general conclusions can be formulated.

SPECIFIC CONCLUSIONS

There are trigger points of recognition that let us know at a glance which figures are completely modular, which are partially modular, and which do not take modularity into account at all. As a final review, study the following list of examples of exterior dimensions in the three categories.

1. **Completely modular:** all the 4' multiples. 4, 8, 12, 16, 20, 24, 28, 32, 36, 40, 44, 48, 52, 56, 60, and so on.
2. **Semimodular:** feet and inches figures other than the foregoing that are multiples of 16".
    Examples: 21-4, 22-8, 25-4, 26-8, 29-4, 30-8, 33-4, 34-8, 37-4, 38-8, 41-4, 42-8, 45-4, 46-8, 49-4, 50-8, 53-4, 54-8, 57-4, 58-8, and so on.
3. **Nonmodular:** any dimension whose feet are followed by inches other than 4 or 8 and that does not conform to the pattern in the semimodular list.
    Examples: 25-7, 36-9, 41-5, 46-4.

Note the pattern that exists in the semimodular column. Each of these dimensions has a characteristic that creates uniformity. The odd-numbered feet are all followed by 4″. The even-numbered feet are all followed by 8″. When the major mod fours are put into this pattern, a rhythm of triads is felt. This can be a valuable memorization tool (in the same manner as children are taught the alphabet to music). Let's try it with a beat.

> Forty-one four (1-beat pause)
>
> Forty-two eight (1-beat pause)
>
> Forty-four (4-beat pause)
>
> Forty-five four (1-beat pause)
>
> Forty-six eight (1-beat pause)
>
> Forty-eight (4-beat pause)

Chant the numbers like a march. Start at one foot four and go to 100. Soon the significant numbers are locked in memory.

The nonmodular column is characterized by figures that have no relationship to material size. A key tip-off here is the odd inch. However, the even inches of 4 and 8 are also nonmodular unless properly preceded by odd and even feet, as explained previously. There is one exception to these principles, which is the house plan that specifies brick or stone veneer siding. The overall dimension may include the depth of the brick or stone. It may be an odd figure that includes the sum of each depth of veneer at opposite sides or ends of the house. In such cases, we must look for other significant dimensions from the interior parts of the floor plan to arrive at the actual frame size of the plan.

GENERAL CONCLUSIONS

1. Modular development produces less waste and therefore provides greater economy.
2. Modularly designed structures require less labor cost.
3. The amount of extra time spent on the drawing board to make a plan modular is small compared to the savings that will be realized.
4. It does not require an architect's degree to produce a satisfactory modular plan.

5. Relatively few plans on the market are basically modular.

6. Any deviation from the modular concept will require additional capital outlay (an extremely important factor to quantity builders).

7. Modularizing an existing plan may frequently provide added living space at little or no additional cost.

19 Application of the System

Before leaving the discussion of modular development, a word of encouragement may be in order. To the student who has had no exposure to building, no hands on or visual association, the techniques described in this part may seem confusing or overwhelming. Words are seldom as clear or impressive as action. When you begin actual construction, much of the instruction will begin to fall in place, to make sense. In the meantime, an excursion to as many house building sites as you can find will be extremely helpful. A mental photograph in the memory bank can be drawn out and examined over and over. Take along a tape measure, preferably one that is 16' long or more. Check out spacings and material sizes. See if the framework adheres to the modular concept. Begin the eyes-on experience. It will be very helpful when you begin to sketch your own design and again when you assist at laying out and assembling the real materials.

For those readers who have had some experience, the material presented so far will ring some bells. The principles just described are a fresh approach, unique in print at the time of this writing. For those with an increasing desire and curiosity, the author's latest full text on the subject is *Residential Construction and Design: Techniques for the Modern Builder*. This book will round out the technical knowledge for all aspects of actual construction. It will be a valuable addition to the library of any professional, novice, or consumer.

The author's wish is for your continued interest in the subject of construction and that your fondest plans and dreams come to fruition.

REVIEW TOPICS

1. Describe the meaning of modularity.
2. What is a module?
3. What does modulus mean?
4. Explain why it is important for a builder to understand these terms.
5. What wood product is the standard modulus of the construction industry?
6. What masonry product is the standard modulus of the construction industry?
7. Explain what the 3-for-4 theorem means.
8. Explain how a designer and/or builder can use the 3-for-4 theorem.
9. What results from a house plan whose dimensions ignore the principles of modularity?
10. Explain how modular dimensions on a plan can be distinguished from those that are nonmodular.
11. Explain why a 24'-deep floor is a full-mod size, whereas a 26' floor is called a split-mod size.
12. Explain why the purchase of construction lumber is mostly a unit-cost problem instead of a board-foot problem.
13. List three or more reasons why it is advantageous to design partitions to intersect the exterior wall adjacent to a common stud.

Erected shortly after World War II, this all-modularized steel home stands in excellent condition in an area of severe climate variation. Although steel homes did not gain great acceptance, the principle of modularization of materials was advanced by this breakthrough. *Courtesy of Clarence B. Luvaas, Cedar Rapids, Iowa.*

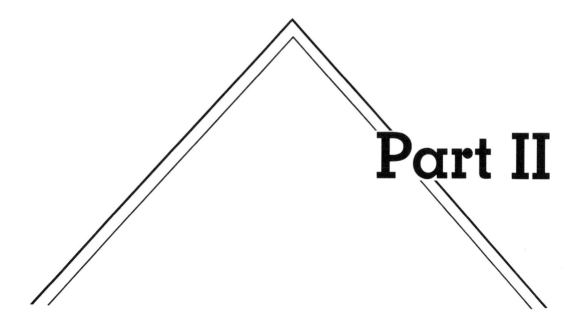

Part II

Drawing
the Modular Plan

20 Importance of Planning

There are many fine textbooks available that teach the art of drafting. Such is not the primary purpose of this book. The main objective in Part II is to pull together the information given thus far into a usable planning skill. Toward this objective, the reader has been exposed to the importance of adequate planning and to the significance of modularity in home building. Not many over-the-counter blueprints are basically planned on modular principles. Few, if any, are dimensional that way throughout. Let us review some familiar planning techniques and delve into the advantages of some new and proven skills.

Conventional floor plans are seldom related to the specific location of the structural components of the floor and walls. In Part II it will be shown how plans can be laid out and dimensioned in a new way that coordinates the plan with the structure. This technique will make interpretation of a plan unnecessary. The builder can follow the plan to the letter. There is now no other known source of the technique you are about to learn. Why bring it into existence? Because it is much simpler. The advantages of a modularly drawn plan are that it:

- Needs no on-site alteration
- Eliminates hidden structural problems
- Is a direct form of communication from the drawing board to the builder
- Requires far fewer dimensions on a crowded plan

As a final persuader, the system has been field tested for over a decade and found to be eminently successful. The author is not naive about the acceptance of a new or radical departure from the conventional. He does, however, have hopes that those interested in more efficient construction techniques and better framed houses will see the advantages that are involved. Perhaps these students will be the first to break out of the old mold. It takes some courage.

21 Floor Planning Principles

In actual construction, a structure rises from the ground and continues on up until the highest part is put in place. There are five basic sequential units of construction:

1. Foundation and/or basement
2. Floor
3. Walls and partitions
4. Ceiling and roof
5. Trim and finish work

Construction progresses in that order. The initial planning of a home, when you are ready to put something down on paper, starts with the indoor living areas. This is called *floor planning*. There are many features and factors that will be coordinated into a total property concept. All the desirable things you want in a home should be written down like a shopping list. When all these things are brought together, the first drawing to consider will be the floor plan.

Begin this part of the assembly task by preliminary rough sketching on ¼″ grid paper. Each square may represent a foot, or 6″, or 3″. Do not feel hemmed in or restricted. At this preliminary stage you are simply trying to put house characteristics and concepts into rough graphic form.

DEFINITION OF A FLOOR PLAN

A floor plan appears to be a top view, as if you are looking down into an open house. It is actually a section view. Imagine that a huge saw cuts through a house horizontally at a point halfway up the walls. The top is taken away. Like the Jolly Green Giant, we gaze down into the open rooms. We see the arrangement of all the areas, the partitions, the doors and windows, the cabinets, the permanent fixtures and semipermanent appliances. The floor plan provides this view and includes dimensions to locate each feature.

22 Room Arrangement

A study of room arrangement should be made from one or more of the architectural planning resources found on library shelves. Only a few basics and pitfalls will be covered here, as the main objective of this text is to coordinate modular concepts into planning.

Three basic perimeter shapes of houses make up the largest percentage of construction. These are the rectangle, the ell, and the tee (Fig. 11). Any other shapes that have 90° corners are variations of the basic three. A tee and an ell sometimes evolve off the rectangle when a particular area in the plan seems too small. A room may simply be pushed out beyond the rectangle, thus creating an L shape.

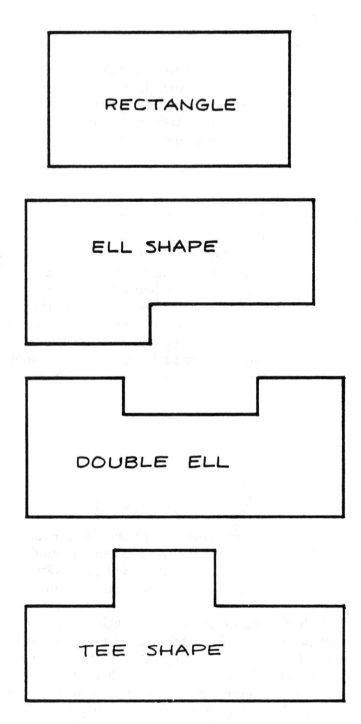

Figure 11 Basic floor plan shapes.

CRITERIA AND RULES FOR PLANNING

The choice of perimeter shape depends on such influences as the budget, aesthetics, climate, lot size, terrain, surrounding houses, family composition, and family living style. The budget will influence the size and complexity of the proposed house. Only so many square feet and so many corners can be turned for a specified amount of construction money. In a highly fluctuating economy, it is wise to plan a structure that will use only 80% of the money available. The 20% cushion will usually be used up by unpredictables. Without such a cushion, the financial situation is usually overextended. Generally, the rectangular floor plan, not in excess of 28' deep, will net the most economical shape to build and maintain. Each additional ell attached to the basic rectangle adds exterior wall surfaces. This drives up the cost of heat and air conditioning.

When attractiveness is the overriding objective and money is no deterrent, any conceivable shape is within reach with only one design limitation. That limitation is found in the roof. Some shapes cannot be roofed properly for adequate drainage. When a plan is really being extended here and there, the planner should attempt to place a roof diagram on it before too much time is expended on interior arrangements. Show all ridges, valleys, and hips. There must be a downhill draining direction for each roof segment.

Considering the climate of the area is important. A study should be made of temperature variations, sunny days per year, and the angle of the sun on the shortest and longest day of the year in the specific latitude. The sun's angle, for example, will have a direct bearing on the length of a roof overhang that should be planned in coordination with the window heights on the east, south, and west sides of a house.

Lot size and shape can force a limited choice of floor-plan shapes. A narrow, deep lot can limit the house plan choices to narrow-fronted styles with rear-approach garages. A hillside plot may dictate a multilevel plan. A high water table can rule out a basement or crawl space and dictate a slab. The laundry, furnace, water heater, and recreation areas normally found in a basement will have to be accommodated in the slab-floor plan. Considerable extra square footage will be required.

Existing houses in a neighborhood will influence the style and shape of your plan. Some conformity of style is desirable to sustain the continuity of a neighborhood. When one house is totally out of keeping with the other homes in an area, it looks out of place and is sometimes considered the monstrosity of the neighborhood. Such a house will rarely bring its full value at sale time, even though the structure is a good buy in every other respect.

Family size and lifestyle are considerations in developing a plan. Children's rooms need to be segregated from adult rooms. A major fault in the traditional American floor plan is the clustering of all bedrooms, with their nearly nonexistent sound privacy. Grandparents need secluded areas. Families that enjoy outdoor eating and lounging will opt for the plan with easy access from kitchen to patio and pool.

Basic planning rules govern where rooms should and should not go. There are criteria from experience regarding sizes, sight lines, and traffic routing. Not all codes cover these items. The emphasis of a code is usually based on safety. Those items that are usually covered in codes are noted in the following list. Other items relate to simple livability. Criteria and good practice rules for floor planning are as follows:

1. An entrance area (foyer) is desirable. A front door directly into a living room provides no privacy. A primary entrance should include at least a minimum sight barrier.
2. The traffic routes should not pass through conversation or activity areas. Alternative routes are needed.
3. A minimum corridor width of 40″ is desirable (36″ is a minimum cited in many codes).
4. Minimum primary entrance door width is 36″ (code). Secondary entrance is 32″ minimum.
5. Minimum interior passage door width is 30″. Minimum bathroom door is 24″ (code).
6. Limit corridor length to the shortest possible amount. Use the wheel-hub concept.
7. Minimum closet depth is 2′ (code). Small rooms need larger

closets. The smaller the room, the greater the need for storage space.

8. Sight access into the main bathroom should not be possible from anywhere except the adjoining corridor (code).

9. A washer and dryer should not face onto a traffic lane (a principle frequently violated).

10. Doors should swing away from living areas and against an adjacent wall so that they are out of the way when in the open position.

11. Minimum window size: 4% ventilation, 10% light (percentage of room square-foot area) (code). Cross ventilation in corner rooms is advantageous.

12. Show kitchen cabinets 24″ deep on the floor plan.

13. The horizontal minimum length of a stairwell is 10′ (more is desirable). Any less length will not provide adequate height.

23 Preliminary Sketching

Sketching is a primary step in the development of a plan. Most people feel that they cannot draw or sketch. If you ask them, they will tell you so. However, if they follow some simple techniques, their lack of confidence can usually be overcome.

PROPORTION AND PARALLELISM

There are two areas of plan sketching skill where assistance is most needed. One is making parallel lines. The other is keeping proportionate sizes. There are methods and tools to eliminate both of these problems.

Graph paper with ¼″ grid lines is an ideal material with which to get started. The most common scale for floor plans on a formal blueprint is ¼″ equals 1′. The squares on the graph paper provide a measuring modulus simply by counting them. To control parallelism of walls and partitions, you simply sketch on top of or parallel to the light green or pink grid lines. Any 8½″ × 11″ graph paper will contain enough squares for a plan up to about 40′ long. A pencil is the only tool needed. One third of a square is about the thickness of a wall. As an example, take the wall-lineup system where the exterior surface of the studs is flush with the foundation. The wall will be exactly 4″ from the building line (foundation line) to the interior face when ½″ wallboard (drywall) is used for wall covering on top of 2 × 4 studs. The actual size of the stud is 3½″. A partition with ½″ wall board on each side will be 4½″ deep. The difference is unimportant when sketching on grid paper. The important thing to keep in mind is that the major modules are four squares (4′). This places the 16″ spacing modules 1⅓ squares apart. The grid makes it easy to visualize the hidden structural members of the plan. This aids in the coordinated placement of partitions, joists, and studs.

BASIC ROOM CLUSTERS

After studying a number of rectangular floor plans, it will be noted that some standard room arrangements exist. Most of the smaller plans (two and three bedrooms) have only a few varia-

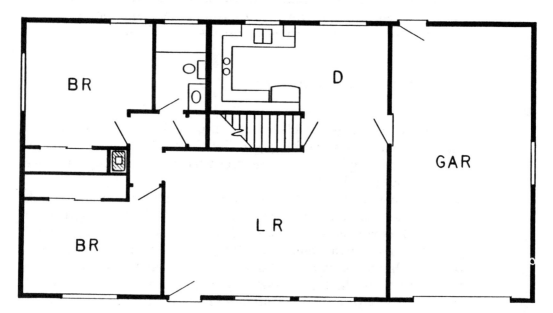

Figure 12 A basic two-bedroom layout.

tions. The living room is in one corner of the house. The eating area and kitchen are in an adjacent corner. The bedrooms and bathroom occupy the other end of the rectangle (Fig. 12). Closets are sandwiched in between the rooms as much as possible so that additional corners do not jut out into living areas and traffic routes. Corridors should be traffic hubs, not long thoroughfares. Stairways and corridors are most efficient at the core or central part of the rectangle, where they pass between other rooms.

Where there is one bathroom, it should be readily accessible from all bedrooms and not too far from the kitchen. Two types of bedroom–bath clusters are most common. One places the bathroom (Fig. 13) and one bedroom side by side on one side of the house. The other bedroom (or pair) is placed across the corridor on the other side of the house. This cluster of four rooms takes up one end of the rectangle. To save money, the bathroom can be grouped behind the kitchen partition in such a way that long plumbing pipes are minimized (Fig. 14). The other variation places the bathroom between two bedrooms at the end of the rectangle. This arrangement is limiting, as it creates narrow bedrooms with all but the deepest-spanned plan.

Sound privacy is an important objective to keep in mind. This can be achieved by placing closets between rooms (Fig. 15). Often they can be designed back to back or end to end in such a way that there is no single wall between any two bedrooms for sound to penetrate.

WHERE TO START

There are two ways to go about the task of sketching a floor plan. One is to use the knowledge just gained and attempt to invent a plan from scratch. Recognizing some pitfalls in advance may be helpful. One of these the author calls the "golden-line syndrome." An idea goes from the imagination to the paper. Some lines appear. Soon there develops a structural or conceptual conflict, a roadblock to progress. The mind goes into negative, subconscious, nonproductive gear. "I cannot accept what I see. I have too much

A

B

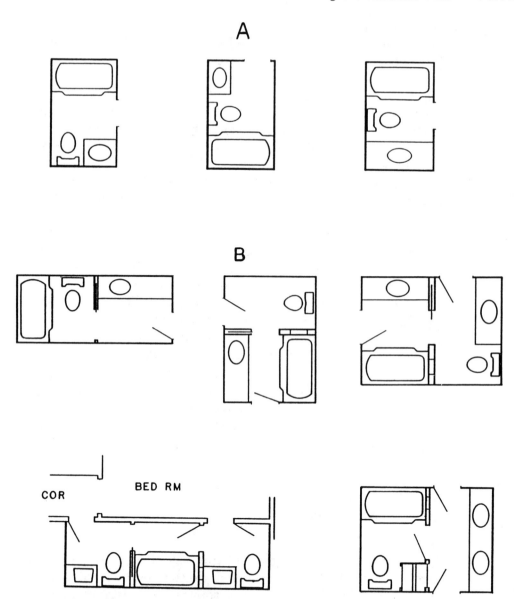

COR

BED RM

Figure 13 (a) Compact bathroom variations for 5′ × 8′ modules, (b) bathroom variations with multi-use privacy features.

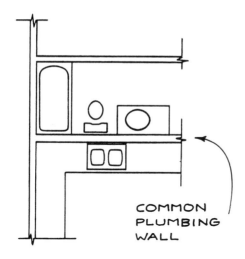

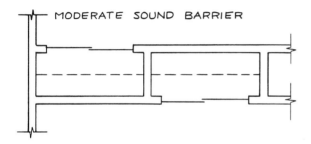

COMMON
PLUMBING
WALL

Figure 14   A clustered plumbing arrangement provides installation economy.

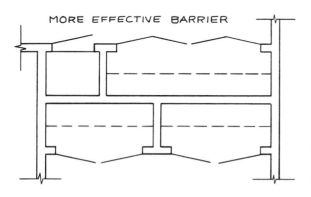

Figure 15   Closets may be arranged to provide a sound-barrier function between adjoining rooms.

time invested to discard it." The tendency is to stick with it in the vain hope that a problem can be resolved or be rationalized away. The lines become very valuable, painfully so. They are your offspring and you will not throw them out. The solution is in the second statement: "too much time invested. . ."

Brainstorm the plan when working from scratch. Plan from the beginning to make four or five fast plans. Stop progress immediately on any plan that is bogged down by the same problem. Start the next trial run. After several attempts, there will be enough plans from which to choose. Keep at it until a potentially successful plan is reached.

The resource-and-revision system is another method of attack. Research is made of all the available plans. Choices are boiled down to a few. Desirable features are lifted from these plans and placed on your sketch. Size and space adjustments are made to conform to the modular objectives. List all the desirable features you want and try to work them in. Soon you have a feasible sketch that is ready for drawing to a precise scale.

24 Drafting the Floor Plan

Drafting a plan that is suitable for blueprinting will require some equipment and tools. Essentials are an architectural scale, a triangle, two or more grades of pencils (hard and soft), and a board with a slide bar or a T square (T squares have been obsolete since the 1940s but are usable). It takes much more manipulative skill to draw with a T square than with a slide bar, but with some practice an adequate job is possible. The cost of these items, including a board with a slide bar, will be much less than hiring a professional to produce a drawing for you.

DRAFTING IS A LANGUAGE

Drafting is sometimes referred to as the language of lines. For simple designing, two primary line widths are used. The object being drawn should stand out boldly so that the shapes of things are very clear (Fig. 16). To produce this effect, a soft-leaded pencil is used. All lines that are part of the structure will be

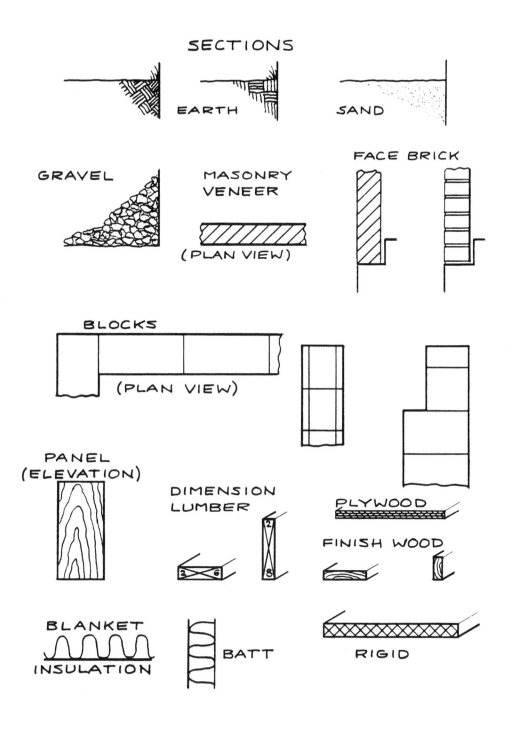

Figure 16 Architectural symbols.

drawn as object lines. Some consistency of line thickness (width) can be maintained if the lead point is maintained at about the same sharpness throughout the drawing. The lead point can be kept sharp longer simply by revolving the pencil in your thumb and first finger as the pencil is pulled across the paper (Fig. 17). Whenever possible, the pencil should be pulled away from your body. This will produce more consistent line thickness. Pushing the pencil instead of pulling quickly puts a flat surface on the end of the lead. Because the point is tapered, it widens as it is worn away. The farther it is pushed, the wider and fuzzier the line becomes. Start the drawing by making all object lines very lightly. This can be accomplished with either hard or soft lead as long as very little pressure is applied. Hard lead is preferred for the first light outlining. Keep the lines just dark enough to be seen. Then it is easy to erase runover corners or to make changes. Heavy-pressured lines frequently engrave the paper and become impossible to eradicate. Also, the light-line technique of starting helps a person to avoid the golden-line syndrome because it is so easy to change lines. The object lines used for

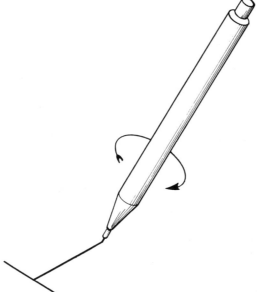

Figure 17 Rotating a drawing pencil improves the quality and consistency of a line and keeps the point uniformly tapered.

walls, partitions, foundations, and so on, will be darkened to their finished width only after all dimensional corrections and changes have been concluded.

Thin lines are used to denote all other features of the plan, such as dimension lines (with their extension lines), center lines, electrical switch lines ("legs"), and notation arrows. It is a mistake to think that line quality is light or dark. Actually, the lightness or darkness comes from the width of the line. For successful blueprinting, all lines must be dark enough to be impenetrable by the light rays of the machine. A hard-lead pencil is used to make narrow lines because it can be sharpened to a finer point, resists breaking, and stays sharp longer.

There are several other qualities of lines as seen in Fig. 18. It will be sufficient for the beginner to master the two-line-width technique. More line qualities may be put to use as experience and the scope of drafting advance.

25 Choosing the Reproduction Method

It is usually necessary to have several copies of the floor plan. This means that an original drawing that can be reproduced is needed. Years ago, copies of drawings had to be made by drafters (tracers). Now this job is done by several mechanical and electronic means. One is the blueprint maker. Another is the copier-type reproducer, such as the Xerox machine. The most sophisticated is the CAD (computer-assisted drawing). The blueprinter does not produce a true blueprint. The name "blueprint" came from the early technique, which produced a blue background and left white lines. The modern white printers produce a white background with blue or black lines, depending on the paper used. Builders and architects still refer to the copies as "blueprints." They are actually "whiteprints."

Inexpensive reproductions can be made by the copier. No special drawing paper is required. Any good-quality white paper can be used for the original. The only serious limitation is the size of the reproduction that can be obtained. Machines that are available to the public in post offices and shopping malls do not

LINE   LANGUAGE

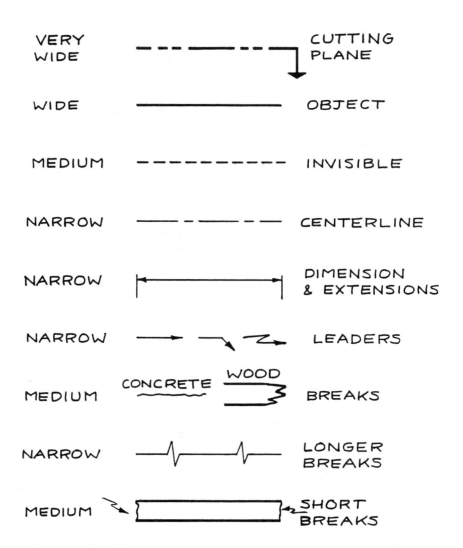

Figure 18 The draftsman's alphabet of lines.

reproduce anything larger than legal-sized paper ($8\frac{1}{2}''$ × $14''$).
Nevertheless, a floor plan up to about $28'$ × $56'$ can possibly be
reproduced by this method. Obviously, there will be no room left
on the paper for conventions or details. Two advantages of this

simple method are a minimum reproduction cost and a very compact plan. It can be stapled to a scrap piece of plywood or carried around the job on a clipboard. The disadvantage is that many more sheets will be needed to cover all the other details and specifications. The disadvantage of more plan sheets is offset by the more convenient carrying size with some jobs.

For those who plan to make whiteprints from the original drawing, it will be necessary to purchase a good-quality vellum tracing paper. This paper is available in several sizes. Some standard sizes are designated by letter. A size is 9″ × 12″; B size is 12″ × 18″; C size is 18″ × 24″; and D size is 24″ × 36″. Note that in each step up, the smaller dimension is doubled. This makes it possible to cut the paper down from D size into the smaller standard sizes. Other proportioned sizes in between these can be purchased. The size of a drawing board to buy, the general size of the houses that will be drawn, and the paper size that will be purchased should all be coordinated before buying either a board or paper.

TRANSFERRING THE SKETCH TO THE DRAWING

Having used the square-counting method on the grid paper, most of the locations that require dimensioning will be well defined. The accuracy of pencil lines on a sketch is not important. The objective on a working plan is to pinpoint with complete accuracy the locations of all corners and openings. To do this, it is necessary to know the actual size of each designated piece of material. Some books on the market today have drawings, mostly details, done in nominally sized materials that are unrealistic and misleading (Fig. 19a). A "two by four" is not 2″ × 4″ in delivered size. It is 1½″ × 3½″. Correct dimensioning is not possible when nominal designations are used. The drafter may label parts by nominal designations but must never use nominal sizes in the dimensions that are placed on a drawing. It must be constantly remembered that the carpenter works with actual sizes, not nominal designations (Fig. 19b).

Dressed lumber sizes were changed in the late 1960s. Prior to that time, nominally designated 2″-thick wood was "dressed" to

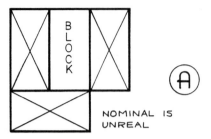

NOMINAL IS
UNREAL

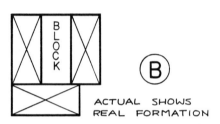

ACTUAL SHOWS
REAL FORMATION

Figure 19 (a) Unreal nominal representations are often misleading, (b) actual scaled drawings are true representations.

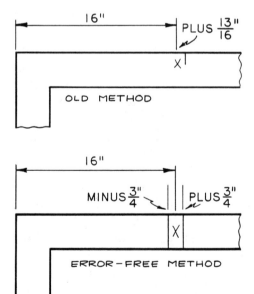

OLD METHOD

ERROR-FREE METHOD

Figure 20 Old-style marking was edge-to-edge. Current marking of both sides is more trouble free.

1⁵⁄₈″ for many years. Today, all mills plane the dimension lumber to 1½″. This makes the job much easier for the layout person on the building crew, because the larger ½″ modulus can be used instead of eighths of an inch. The tongue of a framing square has always been 1½″ wide. No longer is it necessary to draw an edge mark and place an × next to it to show on which side of the mark the stud should be lined up. Now a mark can be traced on each side of the tongue and the stud accurately placed between the marks (Fig. 20). There is no confusion whatever when the stud goes between the lines. Strangely, there was no communication from the tradesman at the building site to the drafter at the board when this lumber size change occurred. Architectural schools did not pick up on the potential that was present in this seemingly insignificant change. Let us proceed to find out how this and our modular knowledge can be put to work on the drawing board.

26 Improved Dimensioning System

Stacked dimensions of significance (Fig. 21) are more important to the builder than a string of irrelevant dimensions whose total equals an overall figure. A main feature of the system about to be described is that all measurements are taken from the same starting point. This beginning point will be referred to as the *zero point* or *POB* (point of beginning). The zero point is most often going to be the corner of the building or another modular reference point from which to take a measurement. The layout person measures from this point. Why go back to this point when measuring for partitions or window openings?

The psychology is simple and proven by experience. Placement errors on the job are seldom made because of an inability to read the tape measure. Errors come in two other ways. One is mathematical error. The other error potential comes from the visual and manipulative limitations of the tools and the operator.

Mathematical errors are common when dimensions are accumulated from one spot to another, to another, and still another. Few layout persons can add a series of feet, inches, and mixed denominator fractions in the mind reliably. Such a problem forces them to do addition with pencil and paper to work out the totals from a starting point. Why do we need singular dimensions from a starting point? When measurements are made by resetting the tape from place to place, an element of inaccuracy creeps in no matter how hard the workers try to be accurate. Experiment with a simple example. Use a ruler to measure a long room. Then use a tape measure that is longer than the room. It is humanly impossible to gain the same accuracy with the shorter measuring instrument. Each time it is moved, an element of inaccuracy is introduced. Every measurement in the construction of a house should be made with a tape measure of sufficient length to go from the POB to the object being located. Tape measures of 16, 25, 50, and 100' are desirable on any full-size house project. Accuracy is the result of operator attitude, an understanding of where error potential lies, and adequate equipment.

See Fig. 21 for examples of stacked dimensions. These di-

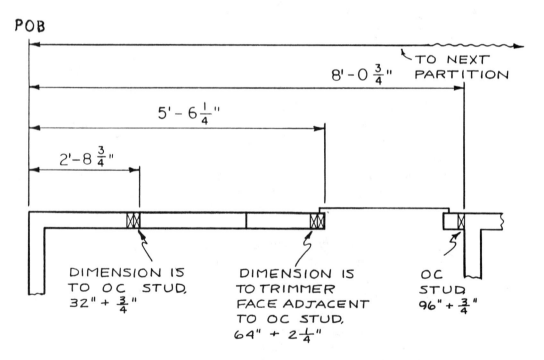

Figure 21 "Stacked" dimensions that originate from POB are more meaningful for the carpenter.

mensions need not go all the way across the house when modular overall dimensions exist (another good reason for modularity). Take a sample house length of 48'. Suppose there were five intersecting partitions and four windows along the wall. Nine location dimensions are needed. An overall dimension can go on whichever side of the house has the least other dimensions. Four of the dimensions may zero point from the left side. The remaining five dimensions may zero in from the right building line (zero point). Remember that using either end of the building line for the POB works only when the overall dimension is divisible by the stud-spacing modulus (usually 16", but sometimes 24" as with 2×6 studs). With this system of dimensioning, a space remains (a room or area) near the middle of the exterior wall that is undimensioned. It does not require dimensioning for layout purposes. It may be dimensioned for checking purposes, although it is not really necessary. Because the plan is drawn to a scale of $1/4$" to 1', it is a simple matter for the layout carpenter to "scale" the distance off the plan with a tape measure. Scaling means laying the tape measure on the plan and finding the distance to the nearest spacing module. One inch on the tape equals 4' on the plan. An undimensioned central locality, as an example, might measure 4" and about $5/16$". At a scale of $1/4$" = 1', a point on the tape a little beyond the $5/16$" mark but short of $3/8$" equals 4" (one-third of a foot). In the example, this indicates a modular room length of 17'-4". The layout person can check this out quickly by counting the stud spaces between marks already placed on the plates. In this example, if the spaces do not check out to be 13 spaces (3 for 4'), there is an error in one of the other dimensioned areas.

A dimension should indicate a precise distance from the zero point to the vertical surface of a partition frame. There it forms a corner with an on-center stud of the wall it intersects. Placing a dimension to the center of a partition creates needless mathematics. There is no logical reason for a plan to focus on the center line of a partition when it is one edge of the partition stud that will be the lineup surface. The choice of which partition face to dimension to, will depend on whether you want the partition in the space to the right or the left of the on-center (OC) stud. This will have been determined at the time of sketching on the grid paper. The same truth is evident for window rough openings. Excess framing is the result of ignoring it (Fig. 22). It is now time to figure out the exact dimension to the location.

NONMODULAR   PLACEMENT OF AN OPENING

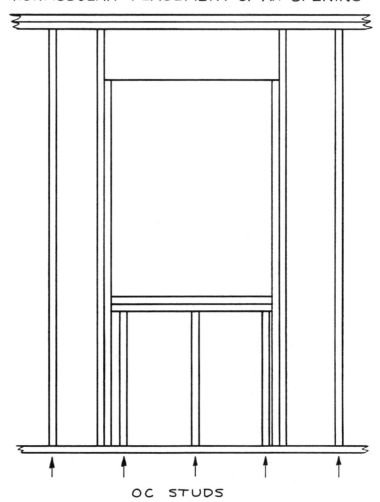

OC STUDS

Figure 22 Nonmodular placement wastes materials.

CALCULATING EXACT DIMENSIONS

Take an example where the first opening in an exterior wall adjacent to the corner of the house is a window (Fig. 23). You choose to coordinate the side of the window that is closest to the corner (the zero point) with the first 4′ modulus point (three 16″

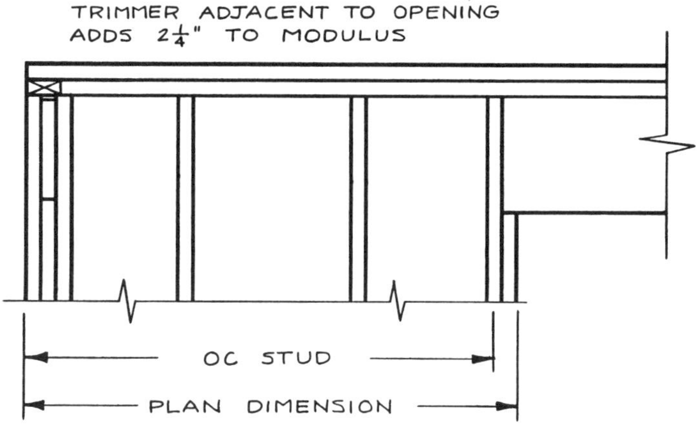

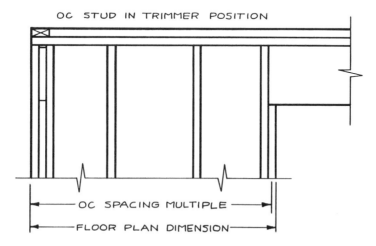

TRIMMER ADJACENT TO OPENING
ADDS $2\frac{1}{4}$" TO MODULUS

OC STUD

PLAN DIMENSION

Figure 23 Wherever possible modularize an opening to coordinate with an on-center stud and trimmer.

stud spaces from the corner). A measurement of 4' from the corner will reach the OC stud in the center of its thickness. The edge of that stud beyond its center will be $^3\!/_4$" farther from the 0 point (half the thickness). A 2 × 4 trimmer is required, nailed to the stud, to support the header over the window. This adds another $1\frac{1}{2}$". The combined distance is 4' + $^3\!/_4$" + $1\frac{1}{2}$", for a total of 4'-2$^1\!/_4$" (Fig. 24). This is the significant dimension to enter on the plan. This is where the opening begins.

OC STUD IN TRIMMER POSITION

OC SPACING MULTIPLE

FLOOR PLAN DIMENSION

Figure 24 Modular placement to a trimmer.

To find the other side of the window opening, a rough opening (RO) figure may be entered opposite the window. The rough opening is the exact horizontal and vertical space to be framed around into which the window unit will be placed. This information will come from the window manufacturer's specification sheet. Take the figures very literally. Do not alter them. There may be two different ROs listed, one for masonry and one for wood-frame construction. The masonry one is larger, as it provides for the window molding to be pocketed inside the masonry. Ignore the masonry RO as it applies only to full masonry walls. The brick veneer house frame will use the frame RO figure. When a spec sheet shows an overall size (OA) for a window casement that is larger than the RO column, it can be assumed that the OA designation is for an opening in masonry. When the RO is entered on the floor plan drawing, the figures must be followed with the letter W to indicate width and H to indicate the height of the opening. These entries eliminate the need to reference to a window schedule.

Framing around a bathtub is another example of special dimensioning on the plan to save material. It is not mandatory to

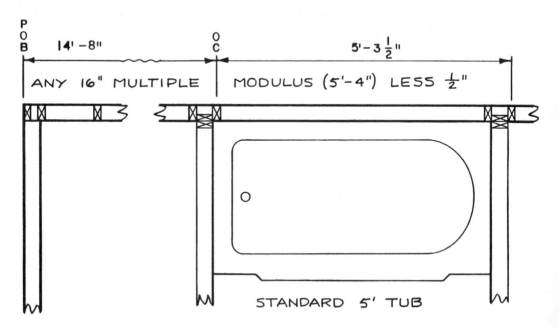

Figure 25   Modular placement of a 5′ bathtub.

place the partition intersection adjacent to a stud in the inter-secting wall, but it presents advantages. Let us take an example where the first partition has been purposely located on the side of the stud closest to the POB that occupies the 14'-8" distance from the starting point (Fig. 25). On the other side of this partition is the bathroom. The tub is to be located against the exterior wall and parallel to it. The tub is a standard 5' model. The tub is framed directly against the stud surfaces, so the opening will be exactly 5' (60"). Five feet is nonmodular; however, it can be mo-dularly adapted to save a stud. When one end of a 5' tub room is coordinated to an OC stud, both ends will save a stud by simply offsetting the second partition ½" on the partition post so that it is exactly 5' from the first partition (Fig. 26). This will not mate-rially affect the corner bearing surfaces on which the wall board is placed. Normally, the nailing surface on each side of the cor-ner that is formed is a stud thickness (1½"). By offsetting the partition ½", the surface that remains on the tub side of the

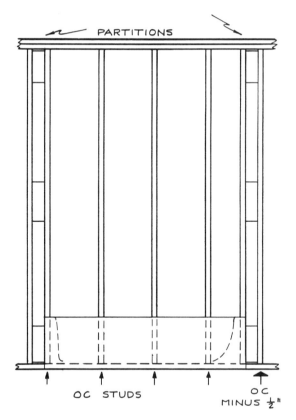

OC STUDS   OC
                MINUS ½"

Figure 26 Move the on-center partition post stud to fit the standard tub opening dimension.

partition post is reduced to 1″. Drywall (gypsum board) should be applied to the exterior wall first (on the 1″ corner surface) so that a full inch of corner surface will remain on the interior side of the corner for nail backing. The carpenter must remember to put the partition at the 5′ mark on the T post and not routinely over the partition spacer blocks, as is customary on other partition Ts.

Closet framing presents an example that puts the partition farther away from the OC stud, requiring an additional stud. This occurs when a single closet intersects the exterior wall at its end or when two minimum-depth closets are placed back to back and their ends intersect the exterior wall. This is a case in point where it is not imperative that a dimension go all the way back to the zero point. The distance is short and standardized. One reference from the zero point to the OC-connected partition is adequate. From that point on, a closet depth dimension or callout is all that is needed. A callout is a specification denoting commonalities or unique features. A common specification callout such as "ALL CLOSETS ARE 2′ DEEP" placed in one of the longest closets will be information enough for the whole plan. Where there are one or two closets of nonstandard depth, the callout may read "ALL CLOSETS 2′ DEEP UNLESS OTHER-WISE NOTED." The layout person finds it a simple operation to lay out the 2′ depth location using the blade of the framing square (24″ long) or tape measure.

The closet that is framed in the rough to a 24″ depth will be slightly less when finished. For example, the installation of ½″-thick gypsum wall board will reduce the actual depth to 23″. A rough-opening depth of 23 to 24″ can be achieved by using two of the 16″ stud spacings in the exterior wall. The space from edge to edge of the studs spanning the two spaces is 30½″ (32″ center-to-center). Conventionally placed intersecting partition studs will subtract 3½″ of space from each side. The remaining RO space for closet depth is 23½″. The ½″ undersize amount can be regained by moving each partition out ¼″ on its partition T post or ¾″ out to produce a 25″ RO with a resultant finished depth of 2′. The gap that results between the post spacer blocks is of no significance.

A deeper closet may be framed modularly by using the two 16″ spaces but placing the partition intersecting studs both on the same relative sides of the OC outer wall studs. They will both be either on the right side or the left side as you face the exterior wall. The 32″ centering is then reduced by only one set of 3½″ spacing blocks (Fig. 27). The remaining rough opening depth is 28½″. With ½″-deep wall covering, the finished closet will be 27½″ deep.

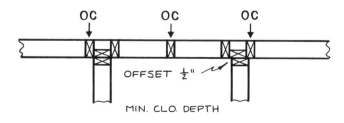

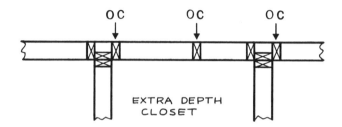

Figure 27 Standard and oversized-closet modular placement.

Both of these spacing systems make use of the OC studs in the exterior wall frame. The dimensioning from the point of beginning must reflect the actual spaces spanned and the real material thickness of the components. You might think that the regard for such precise planning was not worthy of the effort. The misplacement of a partition intersection would be of minor significance. The mandatory placement of an occasional and uncoordinated T post between OC studs is not significant in a house plan if it occurs only in a few places. A complete disregard for modular placement, however, increases cost dramatically when the quantity of window and door openings and the total intersections of inner and outer walls are considered. Added to this will be the waste materials that will accrue from the modular wall-covering materials. Everything considered, the modular planning task is well worth the time and effort expended.

Regardless of which OC stud is chosen for the attachment of

the intersecting partition, the dimension from POB (point of beginning) will reflect a ¾″ plus or minus factor from the modular OC dimension to the stud. The ¾″ figure is half the thickness of the stud. When it is desirable to place the partition intersection on the far side of the stud, the half thickness becomes a plus from POB instead of a minus. Using the same example of an OC stud at 14′-8″ from POB, a partition placed on the far side is dimensioned 14′-8¾″ to the face. Placed on the close side, it will be dimensioned 14′-7¼″. By following this system of plus or minus ¾″ from the modular stud OC position, it is immediately obvious that the partition is modularly placed. Such a plan is extremely easy to read. It eliminates a lot of mental exercise (mathematical checking) and makes layout a simple exercise in association of parts.

WINDOW AND DOOR DIMENSIONING

In the stacked dimensioning system, door openings are dimensioned to the same POB as window openings (the face of the trimmer next to the opening). Only one of the two trimmers can be placed against an OC stud, as none of the standard door widths coincides with stud spacing. The dimension should be referenced to that trimmer so that the modular association can be recognized. Door sizes are standardized. Rough openings for exterior doors need to be 2½″ larger than the finished door. For interior doors, the opening will be 2″ wider than the door. Therefore, it is unnecessary to dimension the width of the opening or to dimension both sides from a reference point (zero point). Whenever it is possible to place one side of the opening next to an OC stud, it may be dimensioned in the same way as described for window openings, the sum of the spaces plus 2¼″ (half a stud plus the trimmer thickness). Should a design call for a doorway to be precisely centered in an entrance or foyer, no dimension line is required. In fact it is undesirable. A simple center line is drawn through the opening into the area in which it is to be centered (Fig. 28). The door width is indicated in feet and inches parallel to the door symbol line. The layout person will have no difficulty laying out the opening. One simply lays out the two partitions, finds the center point between them, and marks off half the rough opening to the right and left of the center point.

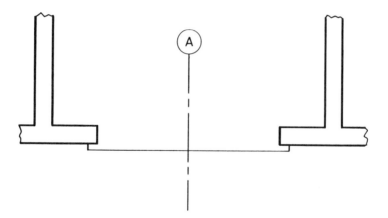

Figure 28   A center line in the doorway indicates a door centered
in a corridor.

There is a lot of unnecessary dimensioning and duplication
on conventional blueprints. Door dimensions are an example.
Most interior passage doors are of the same width (30″). It is only
necessary to label the exceptional doors (those that are different).
A callout can designate all others. It is a waste of time and space
to enter the height of standard doors. All regular home doors are
currently standardized at 6′-8″. It takes a special order to get any
other height. A notation in the door schedule is all that is
needed. Any exceptions can be taken care of on the plan in the
old way. The conventional way to call out a door opening size is
to give the finished door width and height in feet and inches
without the feet and inch marks. This method was adopted by
most architects and drafters after door manufacturers began the
system. A typical door may be stamped on the edge like this: 2/6
× 6/8, meaning a door size of 2′6″ × 6′/8″. A 3′ door reads 3/0 ×
6/8. You should not confuse 3/0 to mean 30″ or 2/0 to mean 20″.
2/0 means 2′ and 0″. Suppose that we have an unusual home with
a special entrance that has an oversized door 40″ × 7′. It would
be shown as 3/4 × 7/0 (Fig. 29).

More recently, this system has been further simplified. The
dashes are being left out and sometimes the height. All that one
sees is a foot figure and a figure smaller in size above and to the
right, signifying the added inches (Fig. 29). A 30″ door is labeled
2^6. The reader must be alert so that this figure is not interpreted

Figure 29 Coded door sizes on new doors.

as a 26″ door. Similarly a 3⁰ is 36″, not 30″. This system is a step forward in cutting down on the quantity of figures that are needless on a crowded drawing.

Windows have also undergone size designation changes. The quantity of specified dimensions as well as the meaning varies with manufacturers. Some cased windows will have rows of specs across the top and up the side of the window symbol on their specification sheets. There will be specs for the overall dimensions (sometimes listed as "masonry opening"), for rough openings in wood frames, for ventilation opening size (sash opening), and for individual glass pane sizes or total light area. To top off all this description, there is usually a model number that may or may not be coded to the sizes given in the specifications. Other manufacturers have simplified the specifying and ordering task by coding the sizes similarly to the door system. There are aluminum window units on the market, for example, that bear only a name and number. The description "Colonial 3030" with one manufacturer means a window with a single hung lower sash, six or eight lights per upper and lower half, and a size dimension that frames into a 3′ square opening. A 3844 window is for a 44″-wide by 52″-high opening (3′-8″ × 4′-4″). The numbers read in sequence to mean feet and inches of width by feet and inches of height for a rough opening in a wood frame. It is simple and effective communication when you know the code.

Being aware of the differences in descriptive technique makes it necessary for the planner to investigate sources and brands at an early stage of the plan development. Such information must be firmed prior to actual framing of the structure. After framing has begun, any changes will be costly in time and money, patience, and morale.

Interior partition framing should follow some continuity that will be reflected in the dimensions. The studs in a centrally located partition that runs parallel to the girder under the floor should be placed on the same centers as the exterior walls (Fig. 30). This will cause the ceiling joist to bear directly over the stud, which in turn bears directly over the floor joist. Like the exterior walls, the spacing zero point will be the building line, the outside side of the exterior wall. The designer must keep this in mind

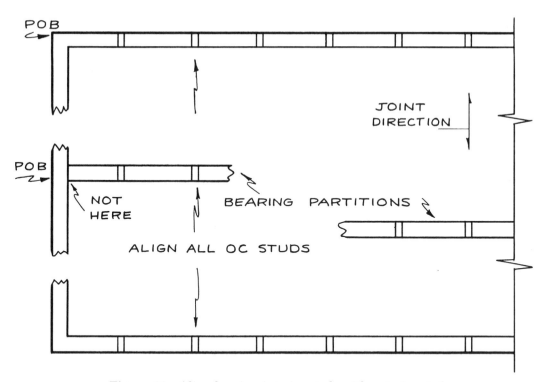

Figure 30   Align bearing interior studs with exterior studs.

when an OC stud is to be used as a unit of a rough door post. The dimension line arrowhead will touch the outer wall at the exterior surface that aligns with the foundation. Doors that are intended to be directly adjacent to an intersecting partition need no dimension whatever (Fig. 31). It takes one stud and one trimmer off the partition face to form the corner and start the opening. The one stud is also an integral component of the partition post to which the door opening is adjacent. This first stud with a trimmer attached comprises 3″ of distance from the partition. From there to the other side of the opening, it is door width plus 2″. When the door is not labeled, it indicates a 30″ door, so the rough opening is 32″.

Partitions parallel to the ends of a house (usually parallel to floor joists) are said to be *nonbearing*. They are parallel to ceiling joists and therefore do not support the ceiling. The studs in these partitions are spaced from the interior surface of the exterior wall frame. Measuring from that surface, the first stud will be against the partition post spacer blocks in the exterior wall. The next stud will straddle the 16″ mark, the next one the 32″ location, and so on. This system should be followed without exception. It provides an index to the location of the studs after the walls are covered. Baseboard, ceiling mold, shelf brackets, and pictures can be installed without searching blindly for the stud. One has only to subtract the wall covering thickness from the first 16″ space. From there on, all the studs will be behind the 16″

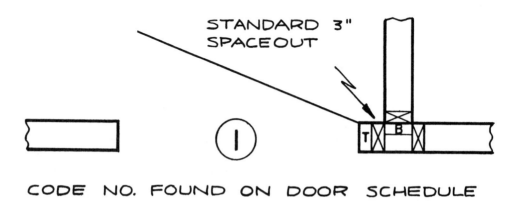

Figure 31 A door adjacent to a partition requires no locater dimension.

modules. Wallboard is placed on the exterior walls first so that an inch of surface remains on the first interior stud to back up the interior sheets of wall covering.

27 Converting a Conventional Plan to Modular

For some experienced designers, the transition from the conventional method of dimensioning to the system just described may be too great a change to make all at once. It is possible to make modular arrangements of structural components and continue dimensioning to the center of a partition. To place a partition adjacent to an OC stud, the dimensional distance to that stud from a reference point will be increased or decreased by 2½" (Fig. 32). The 2½" is the sum of half the thickness of the OC stud plus

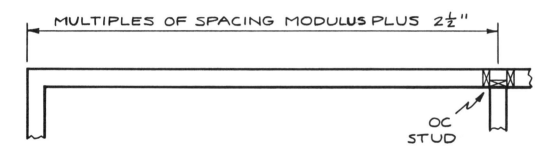

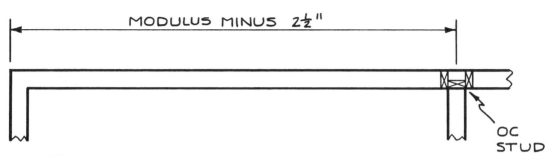

Figure 32 A conventionally dimensioned partition modularly placed from point of beginning.

half the width of the intersecting partition stud ($^3/_4''$ + $1^3/_4''$ = $2^1/_2''$). A 2 × 4 stud is $1^1/_2''$ by $3^1/_2''$ in cross section. Suppose that a designer desires a living room on the corner of a plan to be about 20' long. The adjoining partition can be placed on the far side of the fifteenth stud space (three spaces for every 4'). The actual length of the room from frame face to face will be 19'-9$^1/_4''$. Three-quarters of an inch is added to the interior end of the room (half the stud thickness). Then $3^1/_2''$ is subtracted from the other end (the exterior wall depth). A dimension from the zero point to the center of the partition in this case will be 20'-2$^1/_2''$. From that point on to the next partition center, the dimension will be the total sum of the spaces (modular figure divisible by 16") when the partition intersects on the same side of the OC stud as did the first wall (the far side in the preceding example). When it intersects on the near side of the stud, $2^1/_2''$ will be subtracted. Therefore, all partitions will have one of three characteristics (Figs. 32 and 33):

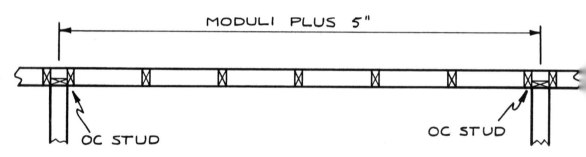

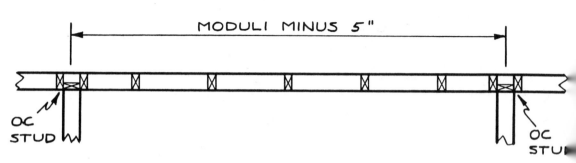

Figure 33 Conventional dimensioning between modularly placed partitions.

- If both interior partitions intersect on the same respective side of an OC stud, the center-to-center distance will be the same as the sum of the spacings.
- Where the partitions are placed on the outsides of the OC wall studs, the center-to-center distance will be the sum of the spacings plus 5″.
- Where the partitions are on the insides of the OC wall studs, the center-to-center distance will be the sum of the spacings minus 5″.

With this knowledge it is possible to recognize a modularly oriented plan that is dimensioned center to center on the partitions. Most plans on the market are not, thus causing waste or revision by the layout carpenter.

28 Dimensioning Symbols

The symbols used to dimension can be a source of pride or embarrassment. It does not require a lot of skill to make them pridefully. A little practice and determination will get the proper result. The telltale part of a drawing that will brand a drafter as a slovenly amateur quicker than any other is the manner in which the dimension arrowheads are formed. Another giveaway is lettering, especially the indiscriminate mixing of capitals and small letters and longhand figures with lettered figures. An objective of this text is to instill a sense of competence and pride in your achievement.

Three recognized symbols are used at the ends of dimension lines: an arrowhead, a large dot, and a slash (Fig. 34). The slash is least preferred. It may be indistinguishable among all the other lines on a drawing. Instead of clarifying terminal points, the slash frequently confuses. Dots are placed dead center over the intersection of the extension line and the end of the dimension line. This does not vary whether the dimension line ends at the extension line or carries on through to another point. The art of dot making is to make them all the same size and round. The size should not get out of hand. Maximum diameter should be about twice that of a typed period.

Arrows take some practice (Fig. 35). Bear in mind two objectives. The width of the arrow fins should not exceed one-

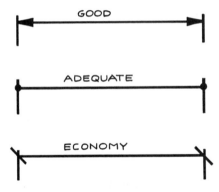

Figure 34 Dimension line terminus indicators.

third the length. The length should be about ¹/₈″ to ³/₁₆″. Start at the intersection of the extension and dimension lines and stay on the line for a little way before starting to flare out. Go back and repeat the flare to the other side of the line. The extension and dimension lines are narrow. The arrowheads may be made with a softer pencil. Even though you stay on the dimension line, the arrowhead will appear darker because it is slightly wider. When you have developed enough expertise to be prideful making single arrows, try some doubles. Change the routine a little. Make the double arrowhead in two passes only. Start on the left side of the extension line. Place the lead point just above the dimension

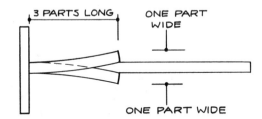

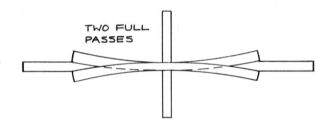

Figure 35 Magnified view of arrow drawing techniques.

line. Sweep down onto the line and carry through across the extension line. Wind up this single stroke the same way you made the upper half of a single arrowhead. Return to the left side and reproduce the motion on the underside. Keep one thing in mind. The arrowhead should be slim and sharp pointed. The flared end is no wider than one-third the length of the arrowhead ($\frac{1}{16}''$).

Dimension figures are made in the printed style (Fig. 36). Longhand figures are never used on any kind of drafting. The figures may be placed in a space, at a break in the dimension line, or $\frac{1}{16}''$ above the line. Above the line is the traditional architectural system; however, it takes a lot more space and may not be practical with the stacked dimension system. Whichever technique is practiced, use the same system throughout. Figures are given in feet and inches with a $\frac{1}{8}''$ dash between. A dimension less than 1' may be given in inches only. Practice is the key to good-looking figures, arrows, and letters.

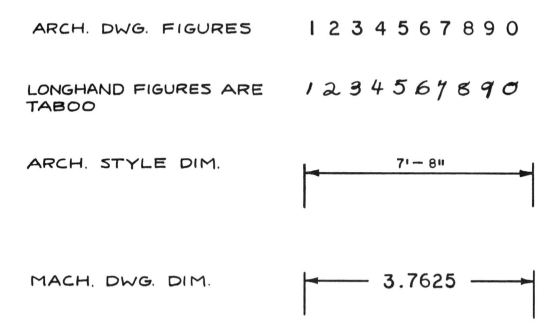

Figure 36   Figure and line techniques.

29 Drawing the Foundation Plan

Now that the shape and size of your floor plan have been firmed, the foundation can be drawn with ease. This is the correct order of planning. A foundation plan should never be made first. That would cause a forced confinement to a predetermined area and make floor planning very difficult. Obviously, the foundation and floor plan require exact coordination. When a floor plan has been developed on the modular principle, the foundation will also be modular. This provides the option of either poured concrete or precast concrete blocks for the building material. A nonmodular floor plan does not exclude blocks for the foundation, but it causes waste and extra labor.

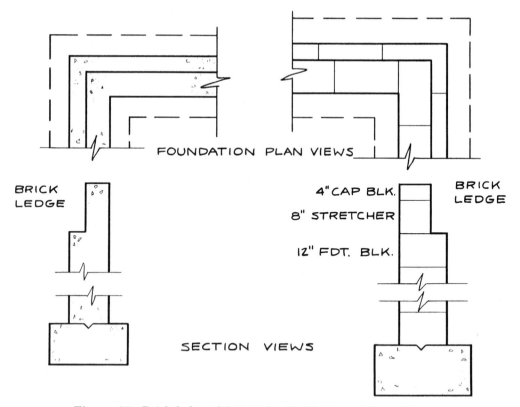

FOUNDATION PLAN VIEWS

BRICK LEDGE

4" CAP BLK.

8" STRETCHER

12" FDT. BLK.

BRICK LEDGE

SECTION VIEWS

Figure 37 Brick ledges fabricated with blocks and formed in concrete.

WALL THICKNESS

The foundation view is taken horizontally through the wall similarly to the floor plan. It is a section view looking down from above. The heavy outlines will show the outer and inner edges of the foundation wall. The thickness of the wall may vary depending on the load it will carry. A minimum thickness for a habitable one-story structure is 8″ (most codes). When a brick ledge is specified in a block wall, the blocks from the ledge surface down to the footing will be 8″ × 12″ × 16″ (Fig. 37). Eight-inch stretchers and caps will form the ledge backup and floor joist bearing. With poured concrete, a 10½″-thick wall with a formed 4″ ledge may pass the code in a particular area. Two-story frame houses (no brick ledge) usually require 12″ blocks or 10″ solid masonry foundation walls. These figures denote minimum practice as found in most building codes (Fig. 38). Local codes should be researched on this point before starting the drawing.

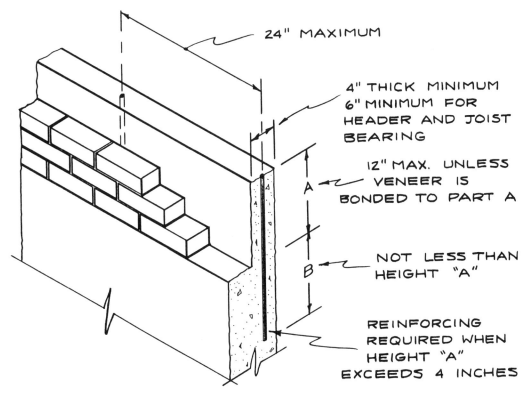

Figure 38 Codes for brick ledge size and reinforcement based on FHA-MPS.

OTHER FEATURES

Several other features of a foundation plan require showing. They are the footing outline under the wall, openings in the wall, and any other footings, such as those under the girder columns and fireplaces. These parts of the foundation are below the sectioning line that represents the main view. They are drawn with an intermediate line width when the drafter chooses to use three qualities of line emphasis. The shape of the line indicates a semi-invisible interpretation. The line is drawn with about 3/4"-long dashes with about an 1/8" space between.

Both sides of the wall footing are shown. The wall is centered over the footing so that an equal projection extends inside and outside the wall. There is an accepted formula for the *minimum-sized* footing proportion to the wall thickness for a one-story structure. The depth of the footing should be no less than the thickness of the wall. The width should be no less than twice the wall thickness. This formula is best remembered by visualizing the diagrams in Figs. 39 and 40. Note that the two stated conditions cause a projection ledge on the footing that is one-half the wall thickness. This means, that in order to abide by the code, the wall must be centered on the footing. Remember that this formula is a minimum standard. It is nearly impossible to produce this exact shape and hold all components in perfect alignment while pouring concrete into forms. It is difficult to

MINIMUM ONE–STORY CONCRETE
BLOCK OR SOLID CONCRETE

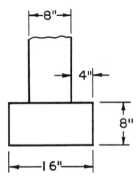

Figure 39 Minimum footing for a one-story residence.

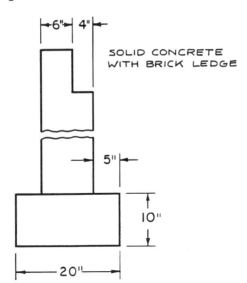

Figure 40 Brick ledge foundation minimum. Concrete block brick ledge combination minimum sizes.

construct forms perfectly. Stakes do not go in where you want them to. For these reasons, builders tend to make footings a little larger than the minimum. This gives some space to maneuver the wall into the correct location without danger of violating the ledge-projection rule. Standard backhoe buckets that dig the trench will control the trench width to some extent. A footing can sometimes be poured without forms in earth that does not collapse. It is common practice to dig such a footing with a scoop of a size larger than the minimum footing width that is required. Keep in mind when drawing as well as when laying out a footing that the footing straddles the wall location, *not the building line.* The wall thickness is all inside the building line. Only the exterior projection is outside the building line.

   Pier or column footings (Fig. 41) are simple rectangular slabs of concrete. The size required depends on several conditions. A conventional roof (nontrussed) will cause more weight to be transferred to the girder pier pads. This extra weight comes from the ceiling of the first floor (in a one-story house). When roof trusses are used, this weight is transferred to the outer walls. It is an engineering feat to determine the exact minimum size of a pier/column footing. Some rules of thumb may help guide the designer who does not have access to engineered

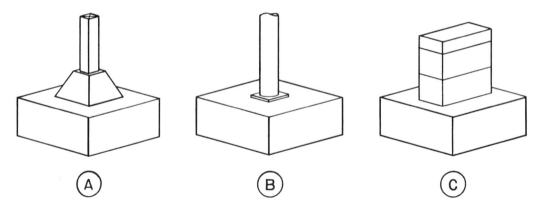

Figure 41 Column and pier footings.

sources. A pad 24″ × 24″ square by 12″ deep is usually considered adequate for a one-story house with columns no farther apart that 8′. The formula calls for the depth to be no less than half the surface width (least dimension). Should the designer choose a little larger surface such as 28″, the depth should be increased to 14″. Adding surface size without adding depth defeats the load-bearing capacity, as the column focuses its pressure at the center of a pad. It can break through a wider pad easier than a smaller one under some ground-bearing conditions unless the added depth is provided.

Locating the column foundation pads with dimensions is done with the use of center lines instead of extension lines (Fig. 42). Only one pad requires dimensions or a uniform callout when they are all the same size. The dimensions for locating the pads will reference to the exact center of where the column or pier will rest. The desired location is a place that coordinates the end joints of the individual members of a built-up girder. All joints should be over a column. Columns comprised of 12′ girder components will be placed at 6′ intervals as the component joints are staggered. All 14′ board components will have columns on 7′ spacing, 16′ pieces on 8′, 18′ pieces on 9′ centers, and 20′ pieces on 10′ centers.

Fireplace and chimney footings may be designed and made as integral additions to the perimeter foundation footing. This occurs when the fireplace is part of the exterior wall of the house. The weight of the fireplace and chimney that is placed on

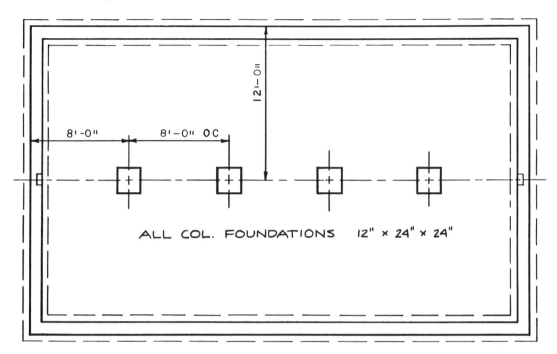

Figure 42   Dimensioning method for column and pier pads.

the footing and the composition of the bearing soil (known as the foundation bed) will determine the size of the footing that is needed. This requirement is so variable that it is suggested the designer seek out professional help before attempting to specify.

Wall openings in the foundation will include such things as a crawl-space access, ventilators, basement windows, and walk-out doors. From a construction standpoint, there are poorly placed openings and thoughtfully placed openings (Fig. 43). Where several openings are standardized, the drafter may dimension only to the centers of the openings. Where there are different sizes of the same type of opening, it will aid the mason to have a dimension to one edge of the opening, followed by an opening height and width stated in the opening. This removes the necessity of looking for a schedule and cross-referencing symbols to find the needed information (Fig. 44).

Openings in basement or crawl space walls made of blocks can actually be laid up with a minimum of measuring when dimensions reference to a corner POB. Openings will be

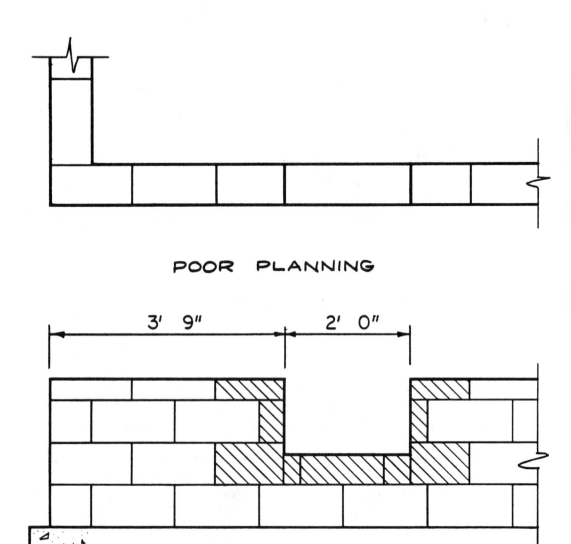

Figure 43 Nonmodular planning causes much on-site custom cutting of blocks (shaded area).

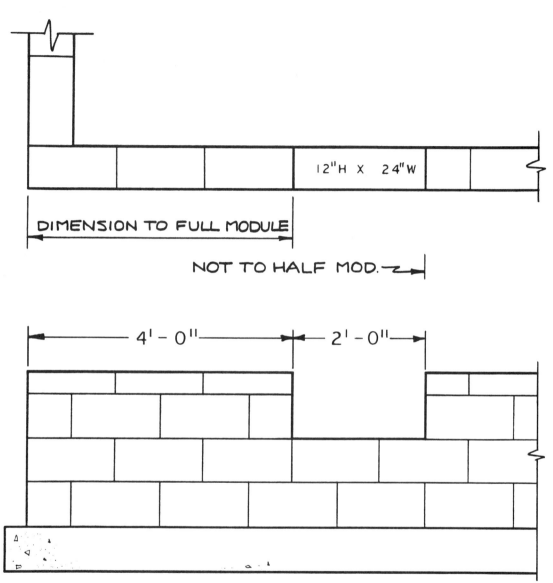

Figure 44 Recognition of unit modulus and good planning eliminate waste of labor and material. Make dimensions as meaningful to the mason as possible in modular terms.

modular when the distance from the foundation corner is a multiple of 8″ (a half-block) or 16″ (a full block) (Fig. 44). The mason can actually leave an opening in the correct location without the use of a tape measure by simply counting units in a lower course. The key to successful dimensioning is to keep in mind how you can tell the assembler of parts (units) where they go or where they are omitted with the least amount of writing and drawing. Avoid the tendency to fill in every blank expanse that does not have a dimension set in it. Only put up those road signs that will get the craftsman to the intended destination quickly and unerringly.

30 Detailing the Floor Frame

Only after the floor plan has been firmed can the floor frame be planned. This is not an essential plan. Many experienced builders will construct the floor frame using only the floor plan. Nevertheless, it is a good problem-solving exercise to draw the frame plan and will be very helpful to the novice. It can reveal the conflicts between stairwells, girders, and foundation openings that sometimes occur. It helps assure that needed double joists are not omitted under partitions or misplaced.

TWO TYPES OF JOIST SYMBOLS

There are two graphic forms for showing the floor frame. One is the single-line representation, and the other is the full-thickness presentation.

The single-line technique is used when drawing space is at a premium and small scale is desirable. It is symbolic. The spacing shown is actual size (to scale), but the thickness of the dimension lumber (1½″) is represented with a single line. Whenever two lines are side by side, it is interpreted as two boards. This can be a little confusing, as the average print reader of details is conditioned to larger details, where both edges of a board are shown. Once the concept is understood, the drawing pace will move along rapidly. Drawing the single-line representation (Fig. 45) will cause less strain on the eyes and the patience than the full-thickness drawing. For every actual board, a line is shown. A

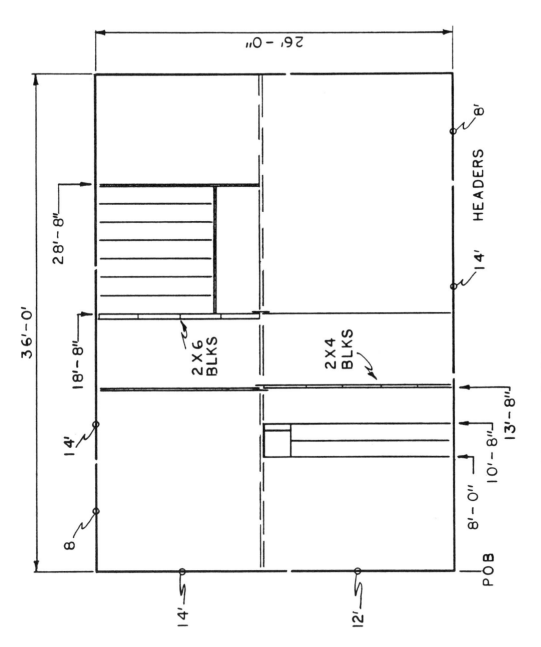

Figure 45 Single-line joist plan representation.

gap is left at points where the end of one board meets the end of another. Without the gap it would appear to be one piece. Lapped boards are separated with a little space, as the line is actually a center line of the board it symbolizes. Each unit or feature will be called out with a label in at least one place. Duplications need not be labeled. Callouts will be squiggle-arrowed or straight-arrowed to the item being signified. These are called *leaders*. Labeling will include such callouts as "OC joist," "double joists," "band header," "band joists," "bridging" (with section size or type), "blocks," and "butt straps." A three-dimensional notation of the size is part of the callout (e.g., $2'' \times 10'' \times 14'$ joists).

   The full-thickness representation (Fig. 46) shows a realistic bird's-eye view of the floor frame. The thickness of each board is shown as actually seen. It is more easily understood because it looks real. All thicknesses of the material are drawn to their actual size. *Materials should never be drawn to nominal size.* They do not fit together the same (the nominal illustration is a false representation unfortunately found in many texts). A $2''$ joist is drawn $1\frac{1}{2}''$ thick. A $1'' \times 8'' \times 24''$ wood strap is drawn $\frac{3}{4}''$ thick, $7\frac{1}{4}''$ high, and $24''$ long. Corner joists are shown lapped and butted exactly as you intend them to be. The wood sill under the floor frame is shown with a semi-invisible long-dash line. Only one dash need be shown between each joist (there would scarcely be room for more).

DIMENSIONING THE FLOOR FRAME PLAN

Dimensioning a floor frame should follow one simple objective. Dimension only the significant layout locations. Do not duplicate obviously related positions. Overall dimensions may vary from the foundation. Some plans call for the header box (the perimeter of the frame) to be set in on the foundation an amount equal to the thickness of the sheathing. When this arrangement is specified, a medium-wide foundation line is drawn outside each corner of the frame. Dimensions will originate from this "building line." The setback at the ends is subtracted from the first and last space between the joists. This must be kept in mind when drawing the joists, the same as it is when actually laying them out on the sill and headers. The zero point is the foundation vertical surface and the surface of the sheathing that will later be placed

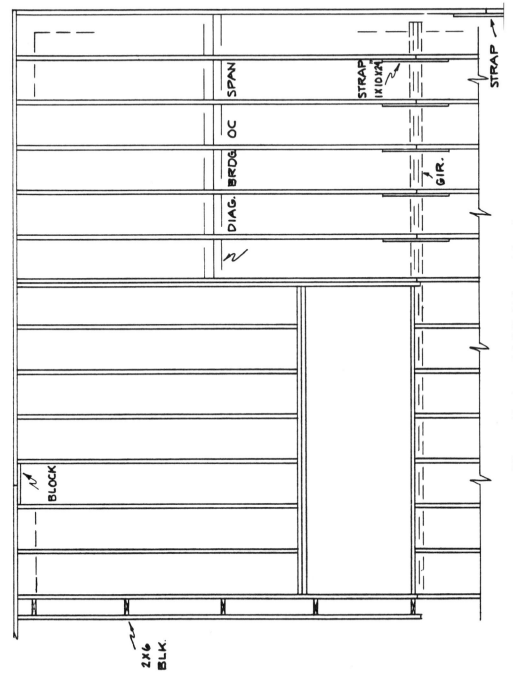

Figure 46 A partial full-thickness joist plan.

81

over the set-in headers. When the specifications call for a header band that lines up vertically with the foundation, then all dimensions reference directly to the ends, sides, and corners of the frame.

MODIFIED MODULAR FRAME PLAN

The objective of keeping things simple and clear can be achieved in the design of the floor frame. A modular floor plan makes it an easy matter to simplify the floor frame drawing. No carpenter needs to see a drawing of every joist in a floor in order to install one in each regular place. What is needed is a plan showing the exceptions. Such a plan is easily drawn in a fraction of the time it would take to duplicate all the OC joists (a 60'-long rectangular house, for example, has 92 joists, including the end bands). Drawing commences by laying out the perimeter box (headers and bands). Next are drawn only those OC joists that are next to any extra trimmers. The extras are those under partitions and alongside openings. To indicate the joist-centering system, the end-joining system (butted or tied), and the bridging (at the center of the joist span), a few sets of regular OC joists may be drawn at one end of the floor. Do not dimension these. Use callouts to indicate the features. Dimensions will be placed to the center of the significant OC joists that are adjacent to the extras. The plan reader can see at a glance on which side of the OC joist the "doubler" goes (see Fig. 45).

A quick way to check out the joist plan (another name for the floor-frame plan) is to overlay or underlay it with the completed floor plan. The doublers must fall under the partitions as planned when correctly located. If they do not, something is inaccurate. When it is difficult to see through the vellum, hold the two drawings against a window pane.

If the drafter has access to a light table, the overlay technique can be used from the outset. A clean sheet of vellum is taped over the floor plan (use a blueprint as the lead will come off an original), and both are taped to the glass top of the tracing table. A fluorescent light underneath makes the floor plan lines clearly visible. Keep in mind that the wall studs of the bearing walls and partitions have been purposely lined up directly over the joists. By visualizing the intersection post, one member of which is an OC stud, the OC joist can be drawn alongside the partition. One side of the joist will coincide with the side line of the partition. The other side line of the joist trimmer to be added will be under the partition. This overlay tracing method makes it possible to locate and draw a major part of the joist plan without measuring. It is a significant time saver and eliminates much potential error.

One caution is important. The dimensioning that follows must reflect mathematical and modular precision. The drafter must *never "scale" a drawing* and assign dimensions. Scaling, in this sense, means tracing something and measuring it with an architect's scale and then dimensioning it as whatever it appears to measure. The actual, full-sized measurements arrived at mathematically and modularly are the only figures to use for real dimensions.

31 Detailing Wall Section Views

In a set of house plans, each view must correlate precisely with all others. Some views cannot be drawn by measurement alone. They must be projected from information gained from a detail drawing. A section drawing cuts through some location of the structure and exposes the parts to view. Making section details helps visualize the relationship of the materials and their proportionate sizes.

FRAME WALL SECTION

Probably the most useful and basic section in a plan set is the wall section (Fig. 47). A complete section would start with the foundation footing and end with the capping shingles on the roof ridge. A view including this much detail could have as many as 50 parts or more to be labeled. It is not usually necessary to go to this extent in order to determine significant heights.

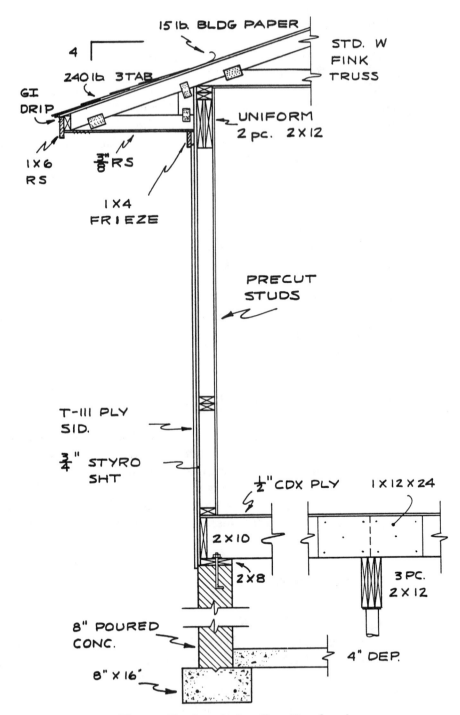

Figure 47 A typical wall section drawing.

SIGNIFICANT HEIGHTS OF THE WALL SECTION

The height of the wall structure itself is controlled by the standardized sizes of the material units in it. When using standard precut studs, the wall height has two possible variable units: the floor joist height and the sheathing thickness. Floor joist height will be greater when the span of a floor is longer (a deeper house from front to rear). For example, a 24′-wide house may require 8″ joists, a 26′ or 28′ span may require 10″ joists, and a 30′- or 32′-deep structure would require 12″ joists. These three nominal sizes are actually 7¼″, 9¼″, and 11¼″ high. Therefore, the house grows in wall height by 2″ increments as the floor depth increases. The three joist sizes mentioned cover all conventional home varieties. When the precut stud is used, the interior frame walls above the floor sheathing are standardized at a height of 97⅛″. The bulk of home designs will have one of three standard exterior heights from the top of the foundation to the top of the wall plate. The wood parts and sizes starting at the bottom are as follows: 1½″ sill plate, 7¼″ header and joist, ½″ subfloor (occasionally ⅝″), 1½″ soleplate, 92⅝″ precut stud, and a 3″ double upper plate (two flat 2 × 4s).

The total height of this assembly is 106⅜″. Substituting a 2 × 10 joist will make it 108⅜″. A 2 × 12 joist makes it 110⅜″. By far the largest quantity of house plans today will call for the 2 × 10 joist, so the most common height is 108⅜″. Where ⅝″ plywood is used for subflooring, ⅛″ more height is added. Because of this commonality it is not necessary to dimension stock parts in a wall section. Each part is called out nominally.

Drawing window and door sections is also a waste of time. Manufacturers supply all this information. The only construction information needed is the rough opening width and height. Where the uniform header system is used (two side-by-side 2 × 12s) over all exterior windows and doors, the rough-opening height is standardized at 82⅞″. This is arrived at by subtracting the height of the header and top plate (11¼″ + 3″ = 14¼″) from the total wall height of 97⅛″ (sole 1½″, precut stud 92⅝″, and double top plate 3″). Door sills of prehung doors are seldom cut into (let into) the subfloor as they used to be when oak was the common material. Today's superior, weathertight, aluminum threshold is installed on top of the subfloor or on top of both the subfloor and the underlayment floor. In either case, the door profile on an elevation view may be shown realistically at 81", as compared to the measured height (80") of years past, when rough openings were cut to be 82" high.

32 Designing the Roof

There are several roof styles from which to choose. The designer should consider the following things before beginning a drawing: the neighborhood styles, the geographic influences (sun, rain, wind, snow, and temperature variation), and building complexity. The average family moves about five times in a lifetime. Some builders feel that resalability merits consideration. Odd designs and mismatched roof slopes are more difficult to sell.

BASIC DESIGNS

Two basic designs make up the largest percentage of roofs being built in the United States. These are the gable roof and the hip roof (Fig. 48). The gable-roof house has vertical walls at the ends of the house closing in the triangular area formed by the slant of the roof. This area is called a gable (Fig. 49). The hip roof slants toward all the exterior walls (Figs. 50 and 51). Other roof designs are modifications of these two types. The exception is the flat roof. It has no pitch (slant), which is the basic qualification of a roof. Other styles, such as the gambrel, mansard, and shed simply combine the slants into different profiles (Fig. 52).

DRAWING ROOF PITCHES

The *pitch* of a roof means the angle of the surface as it rises away from horizontal. In the construction business, this is not given in degrees. It is stated as so many inches of rise above the upper plate surface per 12" of run (Fig. 53). The measuring line is a line on the face of a conventional rafter that is parallel to the

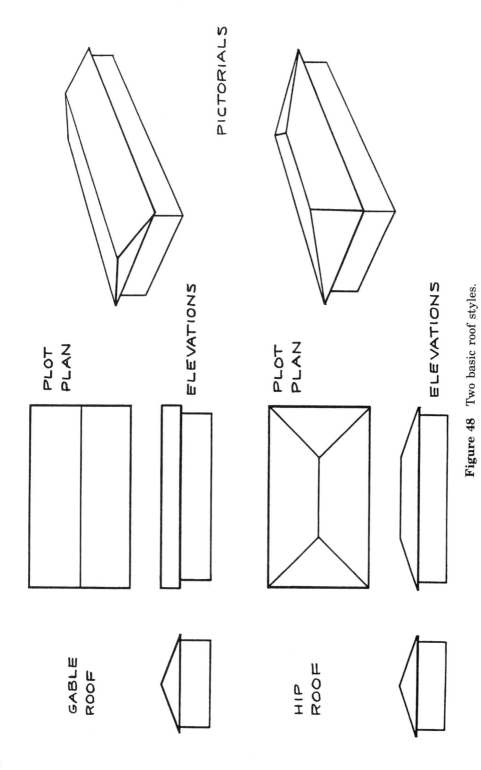

PICTORIALS

PLOT
PLAN

ELEVATIONS

GABLE
ROOF

PLOT
PLAN

ELEVATIONS

HIP
ROOF

Figure 48 Two basic roof styles.

Figure 49 A typical gable roof.

Figure 50 A typical hip roof.

Figure 51 A gambrel roof.

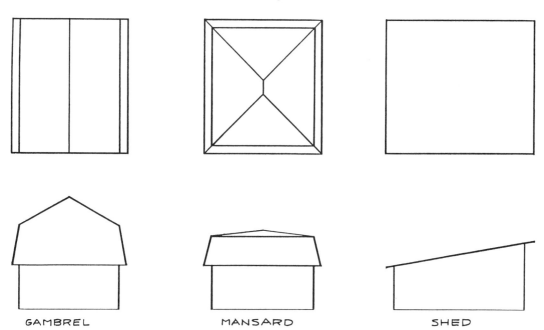

GAMBREL   MANSARD   SHED

Figure 52 Other roof variations are the gambrel, mansard, and shed.

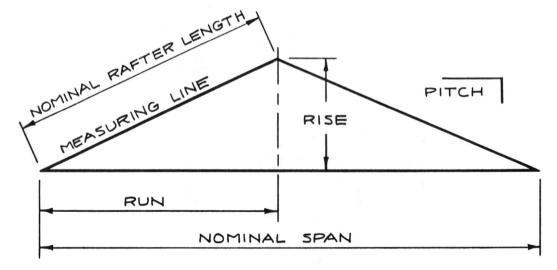

Figure 53 Roof triangle terms.

edges and runs from the top outer corner of the upper plate to the vertical center line of the ridge board. The measuring line is the hypotenuse of the roof triangle. The rise of a roof is the vertical distance from the top surface line of the upper plate to a point on the ridge where the pitch line intersects the center line of the roof profile. The run (Fig. 54) is the horizontal distance from the outer edge of the upper plate to the center line. The span is twice the run or the total distance from the front building line to the rear or opposite building line.

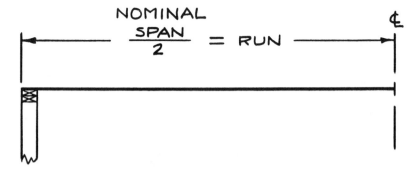

Figure 54 Roof run.

The majority of roofs are laid out and built to a specific pitch given in whole numbers (Fig. 55). The pitch designation may be stated as a fraction or as a set of whole numbers. A roof that is 12′ high at the center and has a run of 12′ may be referred to as *half-pitch*. The rise in this case is one-half the width of the full roof triangle (an equilateral). The base line of this triangle is twice the length of the run. The base line distance, which is the depth of the house, is the *span*. To refer to a pitch fractionally, the rise number is placed over the span figure and reduced to its lowest common denominator: 12 over 24 pitch becomes "one-half pitch." All the even-numbered pitches may be stated in this manner. One-sixth pitch, quarter-pitch, one-third pitch, and half-pitch are common terms in use. The carpenter and architect are more apt to use the proportionate whole-number designations. Orally, the half-pitched roof would be expressed as "12 in 12." This means that in every 12″ of run there will be 12″ of rise. This manner of verbalizing is better fitted to the odd pitches. "5 in 12" is more descriptive than "five twenty-fourths."

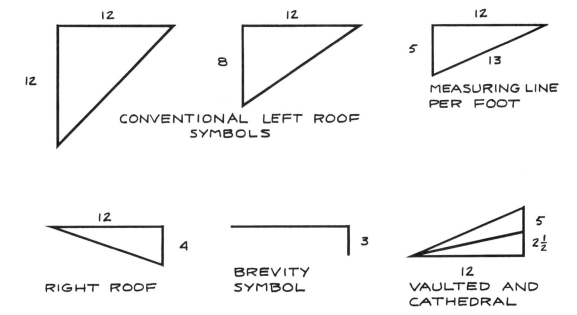

Figure 55 Sample pitch symbols.

The 12″ of run is a *unit of run*. When the quantity of run units is multiplied by the rise in inches per run unit, it gives the actual rise at the center line in inches. A house that is 26′ in depth has a run of 13 units. If the specifications called for a 5-in-12 pitch, the rise would be 52″.

$$\text{pitch number} \times \text{run units} = \text{rise in inches}$$

$$5 \times 13 = 52''$$

House depths that are not in even feet involve fractional computation. The problem for a house depth of 26′-8″ (13′-4″ run with a 5-in-12 pitch) is laid out like this:

$$5 \text{ pitch} \times 13\tfrac{1}{3} \text{ run units} = \text{rise in inches}$$
$$5 \times 13\tfrac{1}{3} = 53\tfrac{2}{3}''$$

LAYING OUT THE RAFTER

To lay out a roof-line detail for conventional rafters, follow the procedure shown in Figs. 56 and 57.

1. Draw an end view to scale of a set of upper plates. The outer edges will be the span distance apart.
2. Draw the roof triangle base line between the plates. This is the underside of the ceiling joist.
3. Draw a center line vertically and measure the actual rise up the center line from the base line.
4. Connect this rise point with the outer corners of the upper plates using a narrow, long, dashed line. This is the measuring line.
5. Draw a line parallel to the measuring line starting from the interior corners of the plates (Fig. 57).
6. Measure perpendicular to this line at the top and bottom of a distance equaling the rafter width (actual size). Draw the upper line of the rafter through these points.
7. Draw in an end view of the ridge board. Straddle the center line. Choose a board width large enough so that all the plumb-cut rafter end bears on the board. This usually means that the ridge board will be one size larger than the rafter.

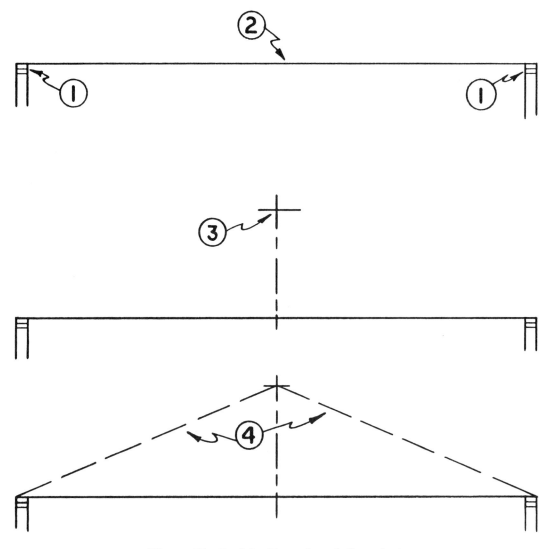

Figure 56   Roof drafting; steps 1 through 4.

8. Measure up from the base line the height of the ceiling joist and draw it in.
9. Draw a horizontal collar beam (1 × 6 or 2 × 4) at a point two-thirds of the distance above the base line. A collar beam is usually required for each 4' of house length.

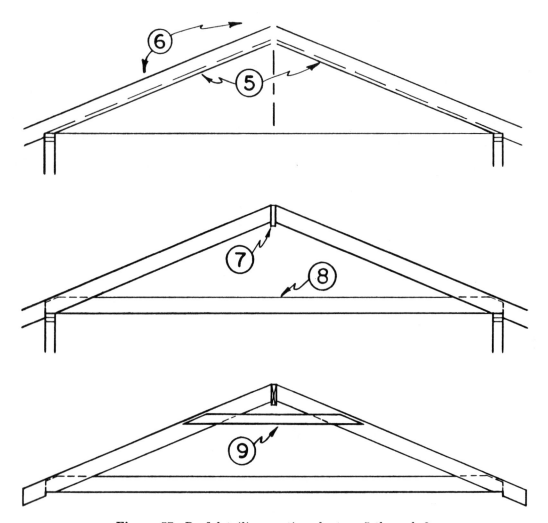

Figure 57 Roof detailing continued; steps 5 through 9.

This is the basic layout for a conventional set of rafters and ceiling joists. Overhangs have no effect on this layout procedure. The overhang is a simple extension of the rafter lines. Overhang and soffit design is discussed later in the book.

33 Drawing the W and the M Truss

The Fink and the Howe trusses, nicknamed the W and the M, are laid out in a similar way. Steps 1, 2, and 3 are the same. The measuring line, step 4, may be drawn in solid, as it is the lower edge of the upper truss chord. The rafters on a truss are called upper chords. The lower edge of the upper chord coincides with the measuring line. The upper chord sits on the pitch-cut scarf of the lower chord. There is no bird's-mouth bearing seat on a truss, as found on the bottom of the conventional rafter. The height of the rafter (its vertical girth) is all above the measuring line. There is no ridge board where trusses are used. The upper end of the chords meet and bear against each other on their plumb cuts.

Placing the webs on a truss drawing is a precise matter. Webs are the tension and compression braces connecting upper and lower chords. The locations have been worked out through engineering principles and stress tests to assure the greatest possible strength. Changing the intersection locations by more than the width of a web board will weaken the load-bearing capacity of a truss.

On the lower chord of the W truss, the webs should be placed on third points (Fig. 58). This means one-third of the *clear* span (the distance across the span from the interior face of the upper plates). This is the actual unsupported span, not the nominal span (building depth). Dividing the nominal span is a commonly practiced error in design. The webs adjacent to the center will meet at the peak. The outer webs will contact the upper chord at quarter-points. Quarter-points are locations one-fourth and three-fourths of the way across the clear span as projected vertically to the upper chords. To turn Fig. 58 into a scaled detail, the upper chords are placed above the measuring line and the lower chords are placed above the base line. The center line for the webs will meet the lower chord on its top surface, intersecting the vertical center line of the third point. This places the bearing axis directly over the third point.

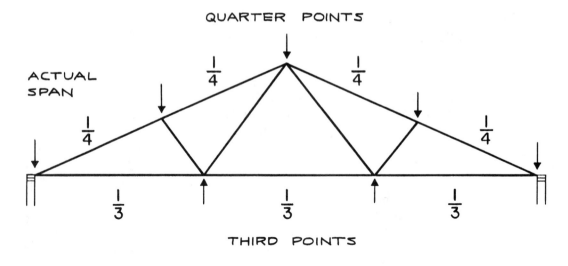

QUARTER POINTS

ACTUAL
SPAN

$\frac{1}{4}$ $\frac{1}{4}$

$\frac{1}{4}$ $\frac{1}{4}$

$\frac{1}{3}$ $\frac{1}{3}$ $\frac{1}{3}$

THIRD POINTS

Figure 58 W truss diagram.

The steps for laying out the W truss are as follows (Figs. 59, 60, and 61):

1. Lay out a set of upper plates.
2. Draw the roof triangle base line by connecting the top of the plates.
3. Draw a vertical center line and mark the top rise point on the line.
4. Connect this point with the outside top corner of each top plate.
5. Measure the depth of the upper chord perpendicularly to the hypotenuse line at the peak and at the top plate. Connect these points to form the upper edge of the top chord (Fig. 60).
6. Measure the depth of the lower chord vertically above the base line. Draw this line parallel to the base line for the lower chord.
7. Divide the clear span by 3 (inside to inside of the plates). Place a short center line through the lower chord on these two third points (Fig. 61).
8. Divide the clear span by 4 along the base line. Project these quarter-points to the top edge of the upper chord.

9. Draw a diagonal center line from the third point on top of the lower chord (not the base line) to the quarter-point on the top chord in each half of the truss. Draw the outer webs by straddling the diagonal center lines.

10. Connect two more diagonal center lines from the third points to the rise point (underside of the peak). Straddle these center lines with the inner webs.

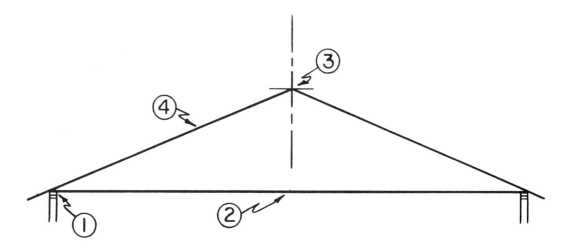

Figure 59 W truss drafting; steps 1 through 4.

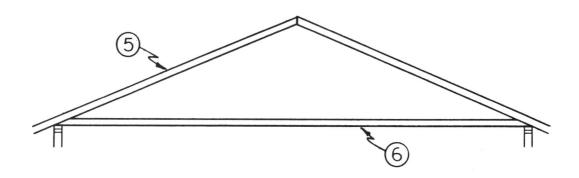

Figure 60 W truss detailing continued; steps 5 and 6.

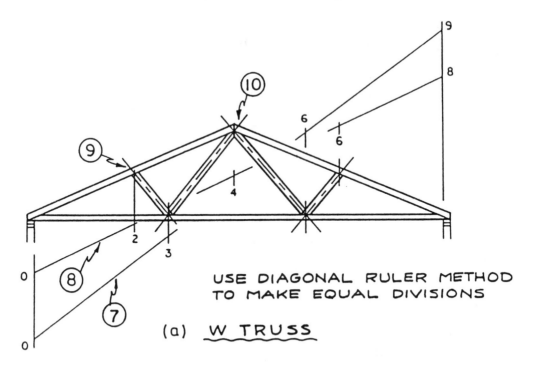

USE DIAGONAL RULER METHOD
TO MAKE EQUAL DIVISIONS

(a)   W TRUSS

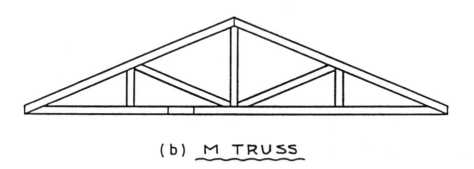

(b) M TRUSS

Figure 61   (a) W truss detailing continued; steps 7 through 11. (b) M truss quarter points are located in the same manner as the W truss (step 8).

Several variations of joint junctions can be made where the webs intersect the chords (Fig. 62). Different pitches will benefit from one or another design. Objectives are to create as few miter cuts as possible at the third points and the peak (the quarter-point intersection will always be a single miter) and to keep the webs superimposed over the center line. Whether it is centered exactly is of less importance than the intersection techniques. Consideration should also be given to the potential nailing surface that will be presented under a gusset that holds the joint in place. Too sharp a pointed end on the web will make for a poor nail anchoring and gluing surface. Where nail plates or gang nails are used, inadequate holding may also result.

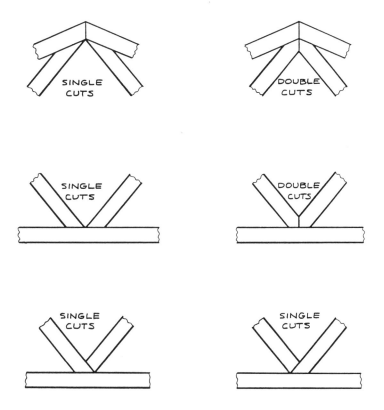

Figure 62 Web joint variations.

The M truss has three vertical posts. The one in the center is called the *king post*. Two smaller ones at the quarter-point locations are called *queen posts*. A web on each side runs diagonally from the top of the queen post to the bottom of the king post. The quarter points are placed the same way as described for the W truss. All posts straddle their center lines. Web ends may be varied from the diagonal line as described for the W truss. The lower ends should bear against the lower chord completely or partially and not solely against the king post (Fig. 61b).

Large wood gussets will cover the members at the intersection points when center lines intersect at the base line. A smaller metal gusset will not. For this reason, one of the standard joint layout variations is to raise the lower-chord center line point to the top edge of the lower chord instead of the base line (Fig. 63). This will make the joint intersection more compact.

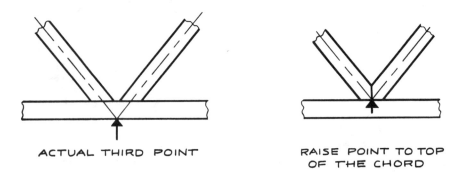

ACTUAL THIRD POINT   RAISE POINT TO TOP
                                                  OF THE CHORD

Figure 63   Compacting a lower web joint.

Where webs meet on the lower chord, they should be directed equally at the vertical bearing line. The amount of fastening surface on the end of each web should be as nearly equal as possible. This will provide an equitable nailing surface for each web. The web center lines may contact the third- and quarter-point center lines at any point along the vertical surface of the chords. This minor variability will not alter the stress properties of the design. This alignment variability permits a design with a junction of webs and chords that is efficient to build.

34 Thermal Truss Designs

The energy crunch of the early 1980s caused both consumers and builders to consider better insulation factors in a home. One key heat loss area that could not be improved simply by adding more insulation was the limited area above the upper plate (Fig. 64).

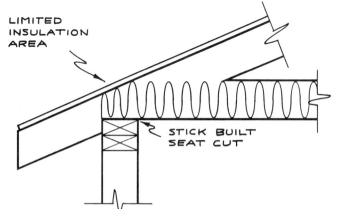

LIMITED
INSULATION
AREA

STICK BUILT
SEAT CUT

Figure 64 Inadequate insulation area with stick-built roof.

The distance from the plate top to the underside of the roof sheathing could be as little as 2″ (conventional rafters with bird's-mouth seats). With 2 × 4 trusses the depth is a shade over 3½″ (the diagonal girth height through the sloping upper chord; Fig. 65). In all but the southernmost states, current recommendations are for attic insulation with R values (resistance to heat loss) between 30 and 40. To gain this level of efficiency, it takes between 8″ and 12″ of insulation depth over the ceiling. Different types of insulation material have different values per inch of thickness. To accomplish this depth over the exterior plate, a truss design with a short cripple stud to raise the upper chord is available (Fig. 66). The builder can request any height of cripple desired. The method is effective but expensive. It requires an additional joint with two more gussets and sometimes an extra web per side. It opens a greater area on the face of the building

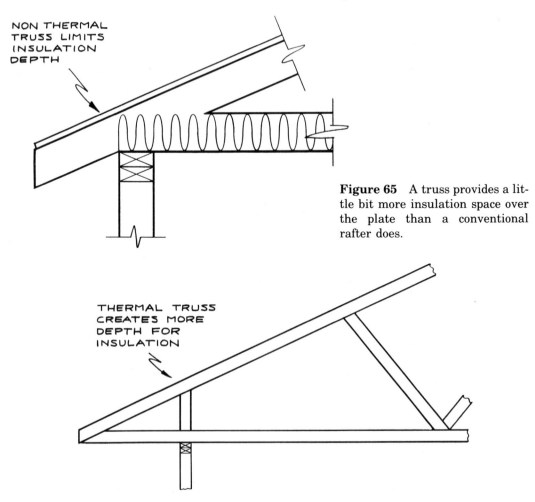

NON THERMAL
TRUSS LIMITS
INSULATION
DEPTH

Figure 65   A truss provides a little bit more insulation space over the plate than a conventional rafter does.

THERMAL TRUSS
CREATES MORE
DEPTH FOR
INSULATION

Figure 66   Cripple stud thermal truss design.

above the plate, which must be sheathed to contain the insulation. When early American homes had open rafters tails, this closure piece was called a bird stop. It can now be more appropriately referred to as an *insulation stop*.

EXTENDED LOWER CHORD

Another simple way to raise a truss is to extend the lower chord length by 2′ more than the span (Fig. 67). This can be done on pitches of 2, 3 and 4 in 12 without substantially altering the

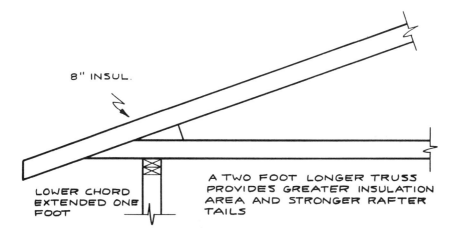

8" INSUL.

LOWER CHORD
EXTENDED ONE
FOOT

A TWO FOOT LONGER TRUSS
PROVIDES GREATER INSULATION
AREA AND STRONGER RAFTER
TAILS

Figure 67   Extended chord thermal truss.

bearing condition over the plate. One objective should be kept in mind. At some point across the width of the surface of the upper plate, we should be able to draw a vertical line that does not leave the surface of the lower and upper chords. There should be a bearing line through the contact point of the chords. When the lower chord extends so far that a gap exists between the chords above the plate, it can be remedied by filling the gap with a wedge. This wedge is ready made from the scarf cutoffs at the end of the lower chords (the rake cut line) (Fig. 68). The wedge is inserted between the chords. A single gusset on each side covers both joints and the wedge. When the economy of this system is explained to the truss maker, it frequently becomes the choice over the cripple design. A truss with 2 × 4 chords will contain about 8″ of cavity above the plate with this design. Another variation of this design is to use a lower chord 4′ longer than the span. With a 2′ overhang (Fig. 69), this design provides a ready-made soffit nailing framework. Cut the wedge block from the scarf-cut end of the top chord. Coordinate the design with a facia backer for a completely modular overhang (Fig. 70). Still another variation uses span-length chords with a simple custom-cut wedge (Fig. 71).

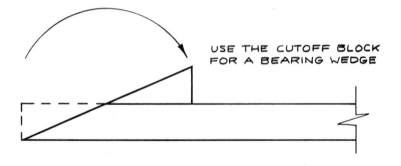

USE THE CUTOFF BLOCK
FOR A BEARING WEDGE

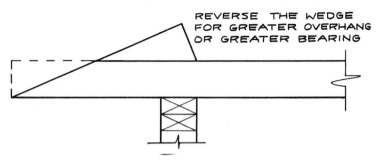

REVERSE THE WEDGE
FOR GREATER OVERHANG
OR GREATER BEARING

Figure 68 A filler wedge.

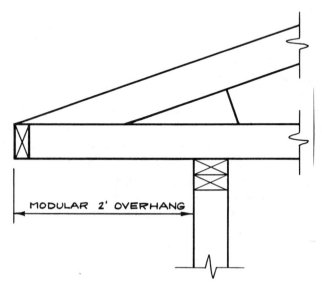

MODULAR 2' OVERHANG

Figure 69 Modular plancier overhang truss.

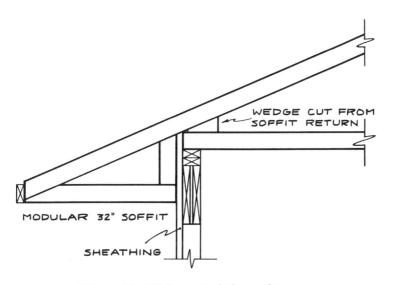

Figure 70 Wedge-raised thermal truss.

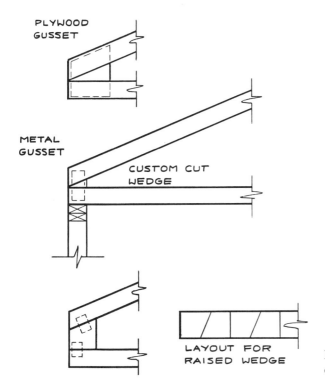

Figure 71 Thermal truss with conventional height soffit.

35 Roof Venting Modules

Building codes usually prescribe the minimum ventilation area in terms of proportion to the square footage of the ceiling or attic. The Federal Housing Administration (FHA) requires 1 square foot of free venting area to every 150 square feet of ceiling. A 1500-square-foot house will require 10 square feet of free vent, area. At least 50% of the vent area must be in the upper part of the roof (at the peak or in the gable ends, etc.). The remaining 50% may be in the eave or cornice. Free vent area literally means no obstruction to airflow. All vents have screening or fins or both. An 8″ × 12″ soffit vent does not qualify for 96 square inches of venting area. Probably 75% of that is a more realistic estimate. It is a good practice to overplan venting area. If the specifications require 12 square feet, 16 square feet will more closely meet the requirement.

Eave vents are important on both gable- and hip-roof houses. It was once thought that they were a characteristic of hip roofs only. Big gable vents are effective when there is a direct air current into one or the other. The suction created on the off-wind end, aided by the pressure from the wind against the other end, will circulate much of the hot air out of the central and upper portions of the attic. It will not pull it up from the eave area to any extent when there are no eave vents. To do this, there must be a fresh-air inlet source. The most efficient source is a fully vented eave. This can be achieved with an on-site constructed, continuous screen or with manufactured venting soffits of aluminum or steel in sheets or rolls. The next most efficient eave vent is the combination of several small vents. These may be placed at intervals down the eave between rafter tails on a rake soffit or between soffit lookout returns on a horizontal soffit. The vents adjacent to the ends of the house should vent into the first rafter space that enters the attic. It is difficult to remove the pocketed air above the ceiling corners unless the vent is directly below the corner.

A planned air corridor (duct) between the rafters up and over the ceiling insulation is necessary (Fig. 72). Eave venting is not effective without some form of retainer over the insulation to

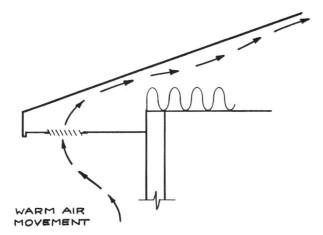

WARM AIR
MOVEMENT

Figure 72   Venting corridor over the plate.

prevent it from closing the aperture. There are several brands of manufactured vent stops on the market designed to fit 16″ and 24″ centered rafters. Stops can be made on site (Fig. 73) with a variety of materials. An effective material is rigid 1″ Styrofoam ripped to 14½″ width for 16″ OC rafters, or 22½″ for 24″ rafters. The length required will vary with different roof pitches and insulation depths. A 1 × 2″ strip, or larger, is nailed to the rafter face flush with the roof sheathing. Below this comes the rectangular Styrofoam. It can be nailed to these reversed ledger strips with four 1½″-long roofing nails. The size of this backer strip should be designed wide enough to create an opening above the stop that will equal the square-inch capacity of the soffit vent that it accommodates. When the duct needs to be kept high to allow more insulation below, it may be logical to make two ducts for each vent below. There are two advantages of Styrofoam for the duct material. The R rating is about twice that of fiberglass; therefore, the insulating space lost to the open duct is regained by the higher efficiency of the Styrofoam. The second advantage is the relatively low cost as compared to hard materials such as ¼″ plywood or Masonite, with their low R ratings.

Gable vents are advisable regardless of what other types are used in conjunction with them. When wind is coming parallel to the ridge, a gable vent is fairly effective. When there is no wind, the effectiveness drops off dramatically. Only the rising hot air close to the ends of the attic finds its way out. Attics with

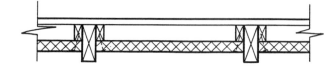

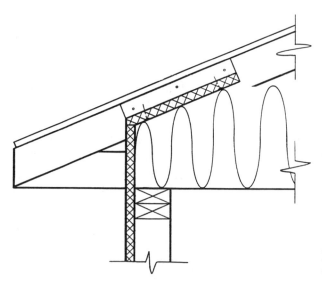

Figure 73 A site-built venting corridor.

only gable vents can run a temperature in the middle of the attic as much as 30° to 40°F above the outdoor temperature. Photographs and plastic items stored in attics with dark-shingled roofs have been known to melt where only gable vents exist. The gable vent also becomes less effective the longer the house is. The air in the attic moves very little lengthwise unless sucked or pushed. The rafters act as baffles that break up the movement. A combination of vents in the eaves and gables is needed to create a circulation by draft as well as convection.

Eave and gable vents are not likely to be enough when a house is more than twice as long as it is wide. Four options are left. A continuous ridge vent is the most effective of all vent types when combined with continuous eave venting.

Static roof vents are available. These are single vents installed over an appropriate 10″-diameter hole in the roof. They are screened and have metal covering to shed rain and snow. The drawback is that it takes too many of them to be used as a single system. They do not add to the beauty of a home and are therefore usually placed on the backyard side of the roof ridge. The static roof vent is effective for a long roof that needs some additional central venting. The static vent should be installed as close to the ridge as shingle lapping will permit.

The nonpowered turbine appears to be working when it turns. In reality, when there is no wind, the movement of the turbine is being caused by the movement of the hot air rising through the fins. Since this air has to push the fins to make them turn, it is likely that the venting air would move out more efficiently if there was no turbine there. The turbine works best when there is some wind to turn it. The turbine is a comforting visual aid with or without wind; if it is moving, you can be assured that hot air is being exhausted.

The power venting roof fan works under all circumstances other than power failure. Its thermostat is set so that it comes on when the attic reaches a specified temperature. The small, fractional-horsepower motor in this fan takes very little electricity. In hot climates this cost is easily offset by savings in air conditioning. A single roof fan should be centrally located where used with eave and gable vents. In the southern and southwestern heat belts of the United States, two or more power fans are desirable. Ell-shaped or tee-shaped roofs could take advantage of a roof fan in each wing of the roof.

Two other options for ventilating or cooling bear mentioning. The gable power fan is an effective exhaust type. The problem with this fan is wind direction. Wind blowing against a gable fan can literally work it to death. A ceiling fan or roof fan, on the other hand, will function regardless of outside wind direction. A ceiling fan can cool a house measurably when basement windows are opened and first-floor windows and doors are closed completely or nearly so. The cool air from the basement is drawn through the first floor before being exhausted under pressure out the attic. The blower on a forced-air furnace located in the basement can also be used to force the cool air up into the living quarters. It is necessary to block first-floor cold-air returns and open a cold-air return in the basement and leave the door to the basement open.

36 Designing an Eave Overhang

Most present-day house designs have some overhang of the roof rafters. The advantages of shedding rain and blocking summer sunlight have caused designers to give more consideration to overhangs. There are structural limitations to how far a rafter may overhang the wall. An economic factor is the 2′ modulus of the rafter length. Adding a few inches of overhang may be unnecessarily costly when it forces the purchase of rafters that are 2′ longer. The same principle applies with the material in the soffit return. For example, if the surface material of the return is to be plywood, a 16″-, 24″-, or 32″-deep return will leave no waste. Size modules an inch or two under these figures will create negligible waste. By comparison, a 36″ return will cause 8 square feet of waste from a sheet of plywood or Masonite regardless of whether it is cut lengthwise or crosswise. This is an intolerable 25% waste factor. The overhang economy will be determined by a compromise of the rafter-length modulus, the return depth (pitched or horizontal), and the soffit material modulus. Metal soffit material, such as aluminum and steel, comes in a variety of shapes, lengths, and widths. The ribbed interlocking type, which runs from eave to wall, frequently comes in 10′ lengths. This length adapts to cutting 15 and 30″ soffit depths (divisions of 120″). Roll types also have specific widths to bear in mind.

ROOF PITCH CONTROLS OVERHANG

How can the designer cause an economical combination of rafter tail and soffit depth? It involves a compromise of several specifications. Roof pitch will have a predominant control on overhang. The constant factor affecting the overhang profile is the level of the top of the windows and doors in the wall. Most contractors are currently using the uniform header, which is made of two 2 × 12s side by side. The double plate laid on top nets 3 inches of height. By adding this to the 11¼″ of header, it is found that the rough opening of the window is 14¼″ below the top of the wall. When conventional rafters are specified, this distance is further reduced by the seat cut in the rafter, which lowers the underside of the rafter tail. The window is likely to have a brickmold or other type of trim board across the top, which also takes up a couple inches of height. There remains approximately 12″ of height (rise) above the rough opening when trusses are used and the lower surface of the upper chord intersects the outer corner of the top plate. This has been the usual method of assembly; however, there are several methods of placing the truss at a higher level to gain additional space for insulation. A conventional rafter will sit about 2″ lower than a truss due to the seat cut. The distance (rise) from the top of the window trim to the underside of the conventional rafter will be about 10″. A line extended horizontally from the top of the window trim intersects the underside of the rafter tail. This intersection point denotes the maximum horizontal overhang that can be obtained. Soffit thickness must also be subtracted when a roof pitch (slant) is steep; the overhang is smaller. As a general rule, longer overhangs may be had with lower-pitched roofs.

Estimating the maximum overhang that is feasible is possible by using a technique of proportion. Practicing this technique may net some satisfaction, as it is impressive. The technique is based on the use of the roof truss conventionally set directly on top of the plate. As explained earlier, the roof pitch triangle from this setup is simple (Fig. 74). The horizontal base of the triangle is the ceiling line, which originates from the top surface of the upper plate. The pitch line (the hypotenuse of the triangle) is the lower surface (under edge) of the upper chord of the truss. These two lines intersect at the building line at the top of the upper plate (this may be the outer corner of the upper plate or the sheathing depending on whether the wall frame has been "set in"). The horizontal depth of the maximum potential overhang can be established within an inch by drawing the detail to larger scale. The larger the scale used, the most accurate will be the analysis. To accomplish this way of finding the overhang, the drafter simply lays out a diagram in the following steps (Fig. 75).

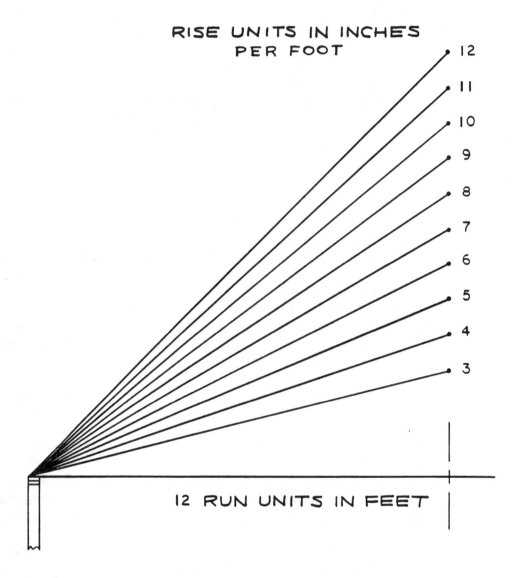

Figure 74 Common roof pitch angles.

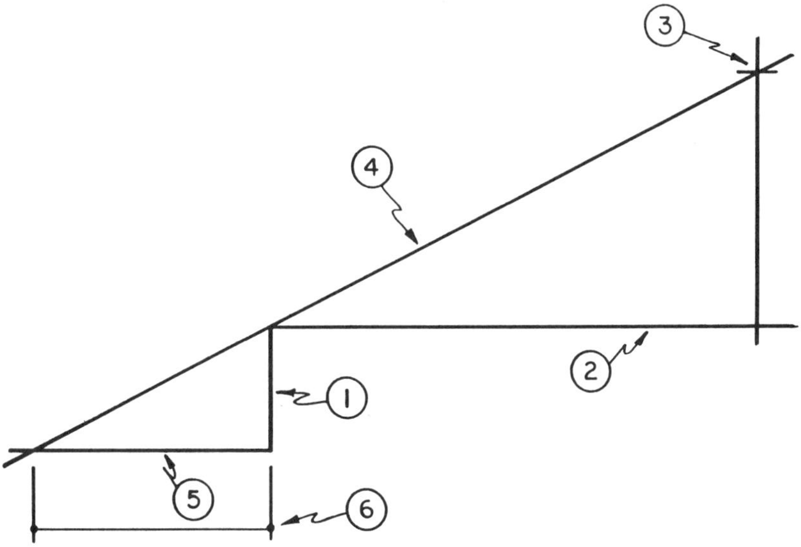

Figure 75   Layout steps for diagramming an overhang.

1. Draw a vertical wall line 12″ high to a scale of 1″ = 1′.
2. Draw a ceiling line off the top end of the wall line.
3. Establish a rise point above any run unit point along the ceiling line.
4. Draw the pitch line through the rise point and through the intersection of the wall and ceiling lines. A truss chord intersects the outer plate corner. A conventional rafter intersects the interior corner of the plate with a line parallel to the measuring line. Allow this pitch line to extend down and beyond the wall line at least as far as the bottom level of the wall line.
5. Draw a horizontal line from the bottom of the 12″ wall line across the paper until it intersects the pitch line. This is the maximum-depth soffit line.
6. Scale (measure) this soffit line. This is the maximum possible overhang using standard wall components (2″ brickmold trim, 12″ nominal window headers, and nonthermal trusses).

This is the basic manner of laying out the section detail. Add in the material thicknesses and heights of the components to produce a finished drawing. Drawings should be drawn to large scale.

The preceding technique is methodical and routine. Another method is mathematical. It is done by mental visualization quickly and accurately—the part that impresses. The key to the process is found in the height figure from the top of the window trim to the underside of the rafter. Place this number over the rafter pitch number as a numerator. Multiply this major fraction times one unit of run (12"). The result is the maximum horizontal overhang. Several of the even pitches can be done mentally (or simply memorized). Others will require a little pencil and paper or calculator manipulation. Following are some examples of both. Visualize a 12-in-12 pitched roof triangle with an eave overhang (Fig. 76). On the house side of the building line, a single unit of run and rise (12 in 12) forms a right triangle whose legs are equal. Extending the pitch line (the hypotenuse of this triangle) an equal amount below the base line and returning it to the vertical building line, we find an identical triangle. The rise of the roof pitch in this example is 12". The rise from window trim point to top plate is also 12". The unit of run is 12". Since both rises are the same, the eave run will be equal to a unit of ceiling run (12"). A formula evolves:

$$\frac{\text{eave rise}}{\text{roof rise}} \times \text{unit of roof run (12)} = \text{maximum horizontal overhang}$$

Let us put the 12-in-12 pitch figures into the formula.

$$\frac{12''}{12} \times 12'' = 12''$$

To show that a pattern develops, try putting quarter-pitch (6 in 12) and then one-eighth pitch (3 in 12) into the formula.

$$\frac{12}{6} \times 12 = 24'' \quad \text{and} \quad \frac{12}{3} \times 12 = 48''$$

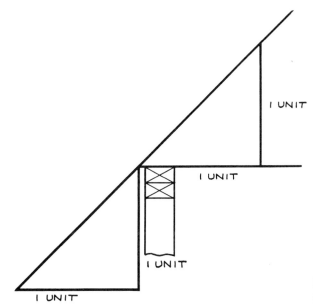

I UNIT

I UNIT

I UNIT

I UNIT

Figure 76   A 12-in-12 overhang diagram.

These three pitches produce perfect modularity of soffit-covering materials that come in 4′ × 8′ sheets (plywood, hardboard, etc.). The overhang depths can easily be memorized by visualization as the triangles are proportionate in inverse order to the numbers:

12 to 12 = 12,   6 to 12 = 24,   3 to 12 = 48

See Fig. 77. Since the numerator of the truss example is always 12 and the multiplier is a unit of run (always 12), one step in the formula can be bypassed. Use 144 (the 12 × 12) as the numerator over the denominator in question (the pitch number). By this simple division, the horizontal overhang maximum figure is reached in one division problem. Some of the pitches do not net even inches. An example is 7-in-12 pitch. 144 ÷ 7 = 20.57″. Converting 20.57″ to the tape measure would transpose as 1′-8⁹/₁₆″. Following is a list of pitches showing the maximum horizontal overhang that results under the specifications noted earlier.

MAXIMUM HORIZONTAL OVERHANG AT SPECIFIC PITCHES

Pitch	Eave rise, in.	Maximum overhang, in.
12	12	12
11	12	13.09
10	12	14.4
9	12	16
8	12	18
7	12	20.57
6	12	24
5	12	28.8
4	12	36
3	12	48

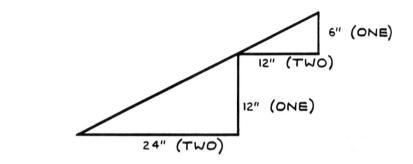

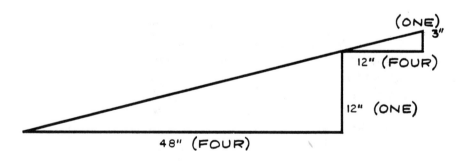

Figure 77   Reverse ratio diagrams of overhang.

Bear in mind that any variable in design or material sizes will usually alter the eave rise number. For example, a high facia on the ends of the rafter tails (one greater than a 1 × 6) will cause a horizontal soffit to return at a lower level. This must be compensated for by shortening the rafter tail and consequently the overhang. A wide frieze board that runs over the windows will alter the formula. Accommodating variations necessitates using the initial formula in its entirety. Two examples follow.

Example 1: Conventional Rafter · The plumb-cut height is $1\frac{1}{2}''$ in the bird's-mouth (the vertical cut of the seat cut). The trim around the window is rough-sawn cedar of $3\frac{1}{2}''$ width (excessive height compared to the short formula). Subtracting these quantities from the $14\frac{1}{4}''$ vertical space above the rough opening leaves an eave rise of $9\frac{1}{2}''$. The specified pitch is 5 in 12. Placing the numbers into the first basic formula gives the following problem:

$$\frac{9.5}{5} \times 12 = 22.8'' \quad (1'\text{-}10^{13}/_{16}'')$$

Example 2: Raised Thermal Truss · The upper chord of the truss design has been placed on top of a square-cut 2 × 4 lower chord, which effectively raised it $3\frac{1}{2}''$. The nominal eave rise is now $17\frac{3}{4}''$. Over the windows, $2''$ brickmold is used. A $6''$ frieze board is desired above the brickmold. The actual frieze height is $5\frac{1}{2}''$. The soffit will be aluminum in a J channel, which takes up $\frac{3}{4}''$ of height. Our computation is

$$14\frac{1}{4} + 3\frac{1}{2} = 17\frac{3}{4} - 2 = 15\frac{3}{4} - 5\frac{1}{2} = 10\frac{1}{4} - \frac{3}{4} = 9\frac{1}{2}''$$

of eave rise. The specified pitch is 4 in 12. Putting the numbers in the formula nets

$$\frac{9.5}{4} \times 12 = 28.5'' \quad (2'\text{-}4\frac{1}{2}'') \text{ maximum potential horizontal overhang}$$

Keep in mind that economy of material use is a give-and-take consideration. It would be foolish to extend a soffit depth to be more modular and in the process cause rafter lengths to overrun their length module to the next longer size. A combined consideration is the objective. All material elements that are affected must be considered.

37 Sun-Ray Control

Control of sunlight entering the home is an important consideration. It has a direct bearing on the economy of heating and air conditioning a home. Frequently, too little attention is given to the orientation of a home. Eaves are designed too short to keep out the sun's hot summer rays (Fig. 78). No analysis is made to coordinate the eave depth with the window height in accordance with the angles of the sun on the longest and shortest days of the

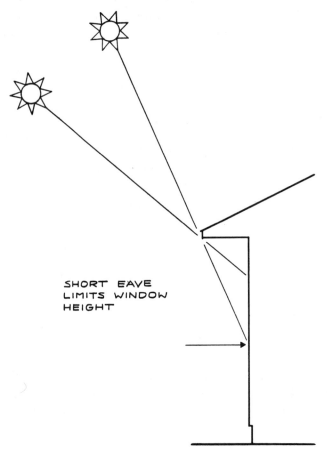

SHORT EAVE
LIMITS WINDOW
HEIGHT

Figure 78 Short eave permits entry of summer sun.

year. Sun shining into the house in the winter to assist the heating needs is a desirable and free solar source of energy. Shade from properly designed eaves is equally desirable in the hot months of the year in many of the warmer climes. To achieve these two objectives, it is necessary to know the lowest and highest angles of the sun in a particular geographic area (Fig. 79). It varies with each latitude. When these angles are known, it will be possible to plot two sun-ray lines on a wall and roof section view. These lines will tell how much overhang is needed to shade out the summer sun on the east, south, and west sides of the house. It will show the lowest point on the wall that a window sill should be so that direct rays of the sun do not enter the house in the summertime.

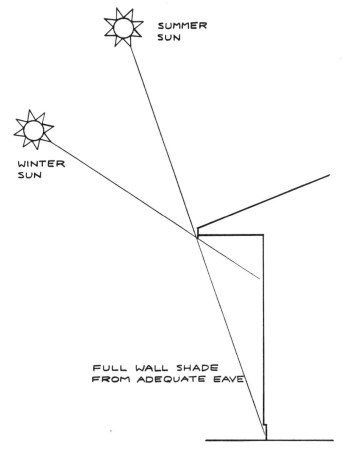

SUMMER SUN

WINTER SUN

FULL WALL SHADE FROM ADEQUATE EAVE

Figure 79 Adequate eave adapts to all seasons.

Consideration of the effects of solar heat have historically had an effect on house design. Short eaves and steep roofs typify northern and New England styles. Long eaves on low roofs, the ranch style, originated in the Southwest, where the sun shines hottest and the most.

Some combined principles evolve from this exercise. To gain a combination of the greatest eave shade and the greatest window height, a low-pitched roof is necessary. Horizontal soffits limit the overhang more than rake soffits. A *rake soffit* is one where a soffit material is nailed directly to the underside of the rafter tails. The rake soffit or exposed tail overhang can extend a little farther than a horizontal return soffit even though the eave drops below the top of the window height. It should not extend to a point that obstructs the view from inside the room, nor should it nullify the light-admitting purpose of the window glass. Obviously, the *rafter tails must not extend so low as to obstruct the opening of storm doors.*

38 Drawing the Rake Overhang

The rake overhang is by far the least complicated type to draw and build. Its simplest form is the open rafter tail design. The tails extend beyond the plate a uniform amount. The opening over the upper plate between the rafters is blocked with single boards or with a notched frieze board. This closure keeps out birds, bats, and rodents. To draw this detail, the drafter extends the rafter lines to a cutoff point that is correlated with the rafter-length modulus and the top of the windows in the wall beneath. The junction of the lower edge line of the rafter with the horizontal line projected from the window top will generally be the limit of the overhang. The exact point will vary a little depending on the existence of a facia board and its height. The facia is a trim board nailed across the ends of the rafter tails (Fig. 80).

The rake soffit detail drawing will start out the same as the exposed tail. It is then closed in with some form of boxing. In regions where wood is still the dominant material, the soffit "skin" may be plywood or hardboard (Masonite). Stained, rough-sawn fir or cedar plywood are popular materials when combined

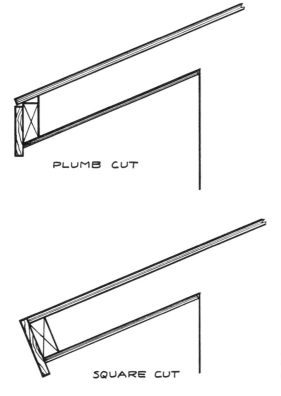

PLUMB CUT

SQUARE CUT

Figure 80 Two basic eave tail cuts.

with rough, square-edged sheathing and facia. These materials do not require beveling. Many obsolete drawings perpetuate the facia with an upper edge beveled to match the roof pitch. Since the coming of metal drip edge in the late 1940s, the practice of beveling has been discontinued. Beveling is not necessary because the drip edge covers all the voids completely.

39 Drawing the Horizontal Eave Soffit

The horizontal boxed soffit requires considerably more time and material to construct. It requires backup materials called nailers upon which the soffit skin is fastened. On a conventionally built rafter system, the boards crossing from the end of the tails back to the wall face are called plancier or cornice frames. These terms are also used to describe short rafters horizontally placed that form part of a gable overhang. When the eave overhang is part of a truss, this short horizontal board is called a soffit return (Fig. 81). Another backup nailer board is nailed to the surface of the wall from one end of the house to the other. The soffit returns are end nailed at right angles to this nail backer. The assembly is put together at ground level in manageable sections. It is hoisted and fastened in assembled sections. The loose ends are surface nailed to the rafter tails. A cross-section drawing of this assembly will show only the sectioned end of the nail backer that is nailed to the house.

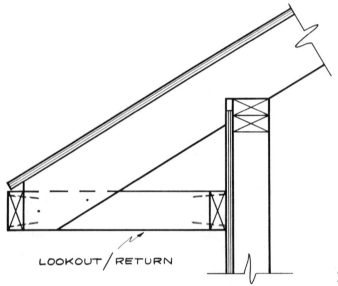

LOOKOUT / RETURN

Figure 81 Soffit framing detail.

The third member of the boxing framework is the facia backer. It is usually a 2 × 4. It serves a dual function. As the name suggests, it forms a rigid backing on which to nail the facia boards. It is a very difficult task to create a straight facia when it is nailed directly to the rafter tails. The nominal 1″ material is too flexible. It requires much shimming and cutting. The use of a backer board behind the facia also provides a good nailing surface on the lower edge for the soffit panels. The grooved facia system is seldom seen anymore (Fig. 82). The routing of the groove is too costly. The high cost of craftsmanship has done

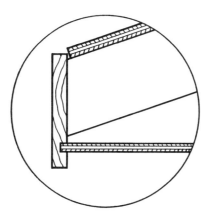

Figure 82 Grooved facia and soffit detail.

away with many good joinery systems in favor of fast fabrication with stock materials.

40 Drawing the Corner Box

The boxed corner soffit (Fig. 83) can take many forms. A primary objective when designing the backup framework is to support it structurally compared to hanging the parts from toenails (the latter method inevitably results in sagged roof corners). A good means of support for the boxed corner is the soffit nailer on the wall face. It can be extended beyond the end wall of the house to a point where the flying return meets it. The fly return, as it is nicknamed, is scarf joined to the underside of the eave end of the fly rafter. The vertical back side of the boxed corner is then flush with the front face of the house.

Another support system may be used when it is desirable to make this corner boxed triangle appear a little deeper. The upper member of the upper double plate on the front and rear walls may be extended out beyond the wall as far as the fly rafter (Fig. 84). This permits the triangular box to continue back along the end wall another 3½″. Some designers feel that this adds to the appearance by giving the impression of a longer overhang (wider soffit). The vertical riser frame piece used to form a nailing backer is face-nailed to the end of the extended plate. This, added to the extended soffit backer, provides two strong members from which to hang the boxed corner frame. The joint at the lower

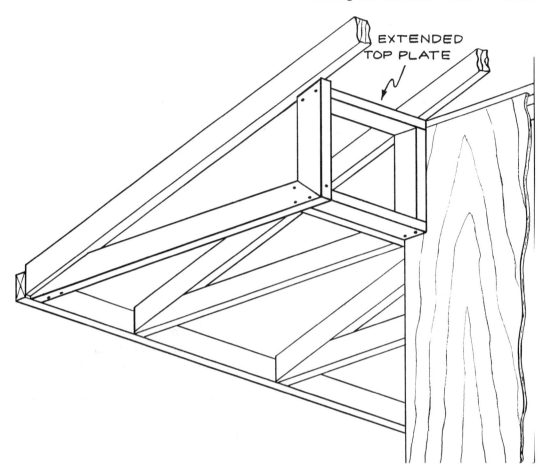

Figure 83   Boxed corner soffit framework.

corner between the return and the riser is a 45° miter so that nails will be long enough to penetrate each piece. A horizontal return to the gable end wall is nailed behind this joint to complete the three-surfaced corner (Fig. 85). All the nail positions in this corner should be predrilled to prevent splitting. A split joint is an inferior joint.

In many homes the triangular facia piece on the corner box is lined up directly below the rake facia (flush fitted). This is a difficult piece of joinery. The slanting upper edge of this piece is a scarf that is cut diagonally across the grains of the wood. Its entire length exposes end grain. The fit must be perfect and the

Figure 84 Top plate extended to support a triangular boxed-corner soffit.

Figure 85 Completed boxed-corner soffit framing. The eave soffit nailer is also extended to help support the bind box.

joint should be glued. This type of craftsmanship is fading away. An alternative design may be used. The triangular facia piece can be neatly recessed. The exterior surface of the triangular facia is made flush with the back side of the rake facia (Fig. 86). It is tucked up under the edge of the rake facia that hangs down below the fly rafter. This system looks neat. It produces a little distinctive shadow line under the rake facia. There is no surface joint to make (no edge joinery to open up when the wood shrinks). Rain and sun will not penetrate the grain and peel the paint or warp the board.

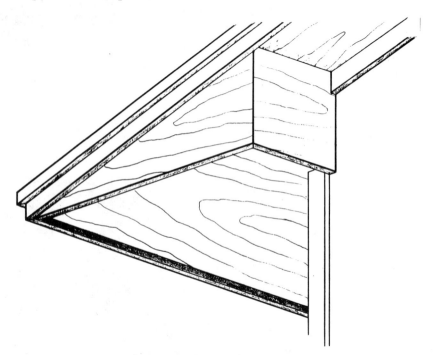

Figure 86   Facia dropback on a corner soffit.

41 Drawing the Elevations

An elevation is a view of a particular side of a house. It is a designer's conception that shows the outline of foundation, walls, and roof. It shows the location of windows, doors, steps, chimneys, and other parts. It must be drawn precisely to scale so that an accurate impression is displayed. It is common to make the four or more elevation views to the same scale as the floor plan ($\frac{1}{4}'' = 1'$). However, if this much emphasis on the elevations is impratical, they can be made to a smaller scale and grouped on the same page. For a very conventional-appearing house, a front view only may be adequate. Elevations provide views to specify some items that do not appear elsewhere in a plan—things such as rain gutters with downspouts and spillpans, chimneys with flashing and projecting flue liners, concrete step profiles and railings, window and door shutters, window and door stylings, siding characteristics, gable and overhang appearance, foundation and roof ventilators, and other aesthetic features.

The technique of elevation drawing is based on measurement and projection. When a height or width is to be repeated at several places on a drawing, it is simpler and more accurate to use the slide bar and/or triangle and project the point to the needed location. To accomplish the projection method, the drafter can tape the floor plan above the elevation sheet. A reproduction is preferred so as not to damage the original. It can be folded to position just the one wall to be drawn. All the vertical lines on the elevation can be projected down with very light guidelines. Next a section schematic of the wall may be drawn to right or left of the elevation position (on the paper or on a separate sheet; Fig. 87). Previously drawn section views cannot be used, as they are usually made to a much larger scale. The section drawing may and should be used as a reference to be sure that no details are omitted. Any omission such as subflooring or a sill will produce an inaccurate and misleading appearance. Floor and ceiling heights are indicated with a few thin dashed lines extending perpendicularly from the elevation. Making the section schematic for projection purposes should not be a lengthy or laborious task. Only the barest bones are shown to indicate heights that project into horizontal lines on the elevation. Heights that are needed for transfer are (starting at the bottom on a front elevation) the footing profile, foundation, grade level, bottom siding line, floor level (to reference door bottoms), underside of window header (to reference window tops), bottom and top of facia, and roof peak.

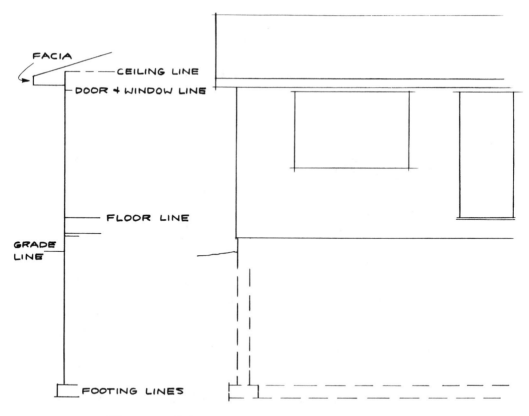

Figure 87 Schematic section to aid elevation drawing.

End elevations are most efficiently drawn by projecting them off the end of the front and/or rear elevation if the paper size and drawing scale permit. All heights are transferable. The drawing will progress at an efficient pace. Items projecting from the roof must be cross-correlated to show the accurate location on both views. Vertical lines on end views can be projected by taping the folded floor plan above the drawing paper in the same manner as described for the front view.

To gain a mental picture of these projection methods, we can visualize a master layout as follows. A floor plan is centered on a large square table. A sheet of drawing paper is positioned perpendicular to each of the four edges of the floor plan sheet. On each sheet a profile view is created by projecting all the characteristics of the adjacent side of the house perpendicular to the floor plan. It is like unfolding a cardboard cube so that each side is on the same plane as the top or bottom.

REVIEW TOPICS

1. Explain why all dimensions on a plan should be based on actual-size materials instead of nominal callout designations.

2. Explain why interior bearing studs should be aligned with exterior bearing studs in a house.

3. What is meant by modular placement of a window or door opening?

4. Can an on-center stud be utilized in the role of a trimmer stud?

5. True or False. Modular placement of a window opening usually nets a saving of at least one stud.

6. True or False. The location of doorways that are centered between partitions and windows that are specifically aligned between kitchen cabinets should not be altered by the layout person.

7. How much should one on-center stud at a surrounding partition junction be moved to accommodate a 5' bathtub that crosses the bathroom?

8. Explain why openings in block foundation walls should be spaced in from the corners and apart from each other a distance divisible by 8".

9. What is the difference between a single-line and a full-thickness representation of a floor joist plan?

10. Why must the drafter be mathematically correct when dimensioning instead of scaling a drawing?

11. Diagram (draw) and indicate the minimum footing formula with the letter W representing the foundation wall thickness.

12. Describe how to place and dimension an opening for a window on a foundation plan where concrete blocks are specified. State the modulus in your description.

13. Starting at the bottom, list all the wood parts of a frame house, from the sill plate to the top of the top plate. Place the actual size of each piece that contributes to the height to the right of its name. Place a line under the last piece and give the total height (sum of the pieces).

14. Name the two basic roof styles and illustrate each with a top view.

15. Explain the difference between nominal run and clear span.

16. From what point on the wall top plates are third points and quarter-points established?

17. Describe and illustrate two ways to design the bearing ends of a truss so that it will qualify as a thermal truss.

18. From a conservation standpoint, what service objectives should an overhanging eave be designed to do?

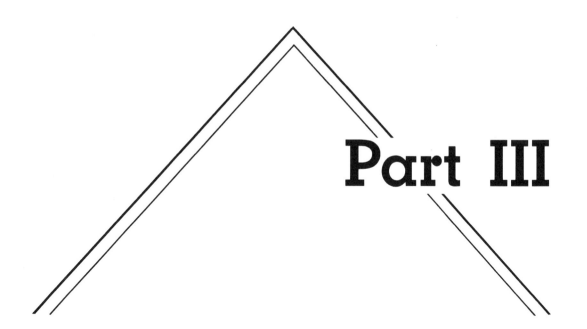

Part III

Stair
Construction

42 Importance of Knowledge

The design and construction of a stairway is one of the more challenging enterprises in the construction of a house. It is a significant part of the house that will affect the comfort and safety of the occupants for as many years as the structure is used. A stairway is seldom constructed satisfactorily without some comprehensive education or training in advance. The inadequate, uncomfortable, or substandard stairway constitutes one of the most common structural errors frequently found in houses of every age. For this reason alone, it is important that novice and professional aspirant alike prepare to understand all the elements that affect the final positioning and profile of the stairs. Because this is an area of frequent faulty design, it is important that learning by copying be avoided. Running next door to see how it was done in another house is apt to result in the perpetuation of faulty design over and over again. Of the hundreds of stairways designed and built by the author, no two have been identical because the stairwell cavity or area is never identical. Designing and cutting the stringers is a custom job for each project. It matters not that the same floor plan is used for a duplicate house. Small dimensional variations will exist from one structure to another. The concrete floor in a basement, for example, will vary in height a fraction of an inch. Any variance in stairwell height or length will affect such things as the bearing proportion of stringer head, the unit rise of each step, the tread run depth, and the head clearance. All these dimensional features ultimately are reflected in the slope of the incline, the depth of foot space on the steps, and whether persons of normal heights can traverse up and down in an erect and comfortable manner. The formulas, tables, and information to follow will provide the necessary knowledge to lay out and construct well-conceived and functional stairways.

Stair construction has undergone considerable change since the turn of the century. Hardwood, custom dadoed stringers with their accompanying treads and wedges are no longer common. Modern construction is typically accomplished with construction-grade hidden parts and covered with finished materials that can

be assembled on the site. The descriptions and illustrations that
follow deal with current practices only.

43 Types of Stairs

There are many types of stairs. The variations are found mostly
in the stairwell or absence of a well. There are *open stair flights*,
which have only the supportive side stringers (carriages) and
treads (steps). This type is frequently found connecting the first
floor to a basement. A *closed stairway* is one where a set of stairs
is sandwiched between partition walls. This type is considered to
be the safest design. There are other innovative designs for spe-
cialized situations. In this category are *spiral stairs* (to conserve
space), *pull-down stairs* (for infrequent access to attics), and others of aesthetically conceived origin. More flexibility in design is
possible with welded steel than with wood. Nevertheless, the
vast majority of residential houses have wood stairways, due to
the lower cost of materials and the facility of being able to custom build them on the site.

The *winder stair* is one that has steps shaped like thin slices
of pie. Steps of this shape may be used to turn a corner with less
space being used than a platform or landing would involve. A
spiral stairway usually has all winder steps. Winders are less
comfortable to walk on. The area of the step that is deep enough
to accommodate your whole foot is usually limited. It is danger-
ous to attempt to walk on any part of the winder step except that
which is deep enough from the nosing (the forward edge) to the
back edge. A recognized advantage of the spiral winder stairway
is its vertical compactness. It can be installed in a square-floor
area of minimum size. For intermittent or emergency use, the
spiral stairway serves a viable function. For regular traffic from
one living area to another, the conventional stairway is a better
choice.

44 Stairway Shapes

There are some basic stairway shapes as looked on in a floor
plan. The **straight-line stairway** (Fig. 88a) is obviously the

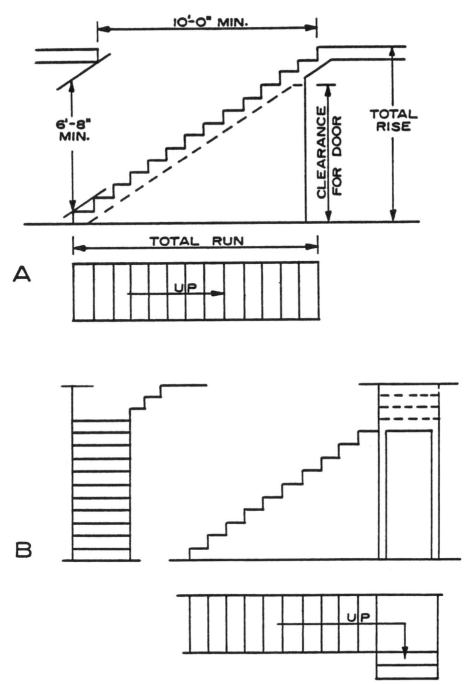

Figure 88 (A) the simplest stairway is straight from one level to another, (B) an L shaped stair will turn a corner by using a landing. The space underneath may be used for storage.

135

most direct route between two floor levels. It is also the simplest and quickest to build.

The **L-shaped stairway** (Fig. 88b) is one that makes a right angle turn somewhere along its rise or descent. The turn is accomplished by making one of the step levels into a platform (an intermediate landing) or by using two, three, or four winder steps to transverse the turn. The landing design is preferred due to its greater safety. An accident victim has a better chance of surviving a fall down a half-flight of stairs to a landing than a fall down a full flight. The elderly and the infirm find an intermediate landing a welcome oasis in the journey from one level to another.

The **switchback** (Fig. 89) is a design that reverses its direc-

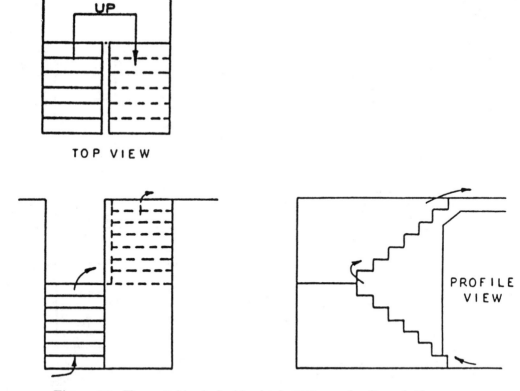

Figure 89   The switchback doubles back 180° on a landing platform.

tion 180° at a midpoint in the flight. Again, the intermediate landing presents the safest design. In this stair shape, however, a significant amount of floor space can be conserved by the use of winders. Whatever amount that could be conserved in the corner by using winders with the L shape can be doubled with the switchback design.

The **U shape** (Fig. 90a) is a combination of Ls. It is practical when some reasonable use can be made of the area between and under the stairway. To conserve the greatest amount of floor footage, steps may be designed in each of the three segments of the U (Fig. 90b). For example, the steps progress upward, then turn 90° at a landing, progress upward again to the second landing, turn 90° again, and progress upward in the last of three flights to the ultimate floor level.

A

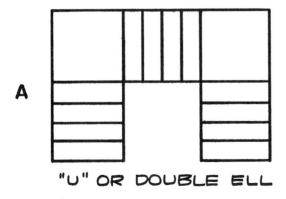

"U" OR DOUBLE ELL

B

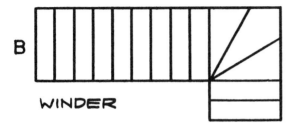

WINDER

Figure 90 (A) The U shape, sometimes called a double L, makes two 90° turns on landings to reverse its direction, (B) a winder is a flight that contains triangular or trapezoidal steps to round a corner.

45 Platform Landings

A landing is constructed much like a second-floor level. It is a miniature floor. To provide adequate head bearing for the stringers, the landing joists and headers are usually 2 × 6s or larger.

One method of supporting the ends of the joists is to lap and nail them to the face of the surrounding partition studs (Fig. 91a). Support, in addition to the nails, is provided by trimmers under the joists extending to the partition sole.

Another joist support technique is to inlet a ribbon (Fig. 91b). The ribbon is less costly in material expense. Another advantage of the ribbon is that it forms a solid backing for any type of wall skin that is applied under the landing (wallboard, paneling, etc.).

A third method is to build a box of headers like the main floor. The joists may be put into the assembly to complete it (Fig. 92). The whole component is then raised into place. It is surface nailed to the partition studs that surround the well. These nails

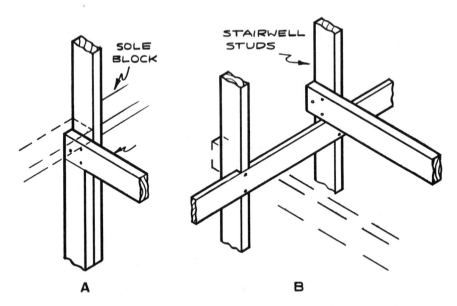

Figure 91 (A) face nailed platform joists supported on stud trimmers, (B) joists supported on an inletted ribbon.

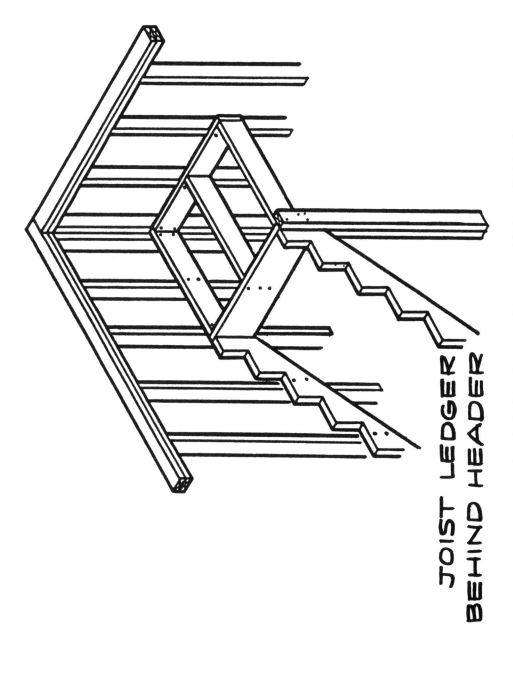

JOIST LEDGER
BEHIND HEADER

Figure 92 A boxed-platform floor may be preassembled or nailed in place to the stairwell studs.

139

should be slanted down a few degrees to provide good sheer stress.

The height of the landing must be assessed carefully. The finished surface of a landing must coincide at precisely the same level as if it were one of the steps. An objective in the construction of a flight of stairs is to create identical heights for each step. This is the modular concept of the flight. It will be seen later, when laying out the stringer cuts, how the top and bottom steps are affected by the thickness of floor-covering materials. The same consideration must be applied to the landing surface height.

46 Stairs to a Basement

There are three common construction designs of stairs from a first floor to the basement level. They are the open stair carriage, the housed stair carriage, and the closed stairway with notched carriages.

OPEN STAIRWAY

The open stairway contains a minimum of materials (Fig. 93). The basic stair flight could contain as little as two stringers and a quantity of treads. To pass a typical building code, it must have a handrail for safety. This, in turn, would require a post at the bottom of the flight to which the rail is secured. Partway up the flight the rail is secured to the floor opening joist. At the top it is secured to a wall stud.

The stringers are of 2 × 10 or 2 × 12 girth. Steps are usually 2 × 12s which net a depth of 11¼". Attaching and supporting the steps to the stringer is accomplished with cleats or dadoes (Fig. 94a). The dadoed type is called a *housed stringer* (Fig. 94b).

The cleated stringer, in spite of its limitations, will often be the choice of the novice, due to a lack of appropriate tooling or expertise. There are some options as to where the treads and cleats may be positioned horizontally across the stringer. Placing

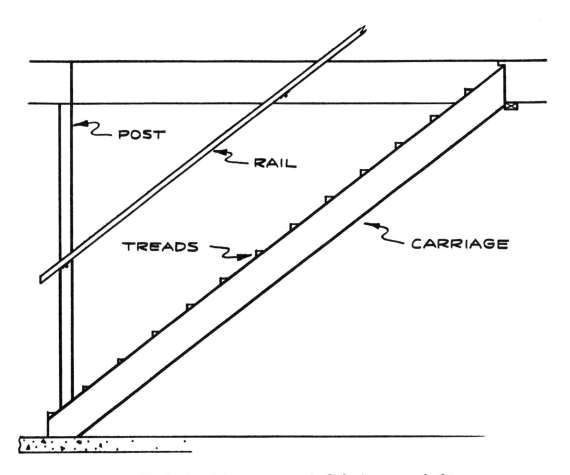

Figure 93 The basic minimum open stair flight is composed of two carriages, treads, a hand rail, and a rail post.

them close to the back of the stringer has an advantage in that the front top sides of the stringer protrude beyond the treads, thereby providing a little curbing. Small as it is, this curbing is helpful to toddlers or persons who may need to feel the identity of the boundaries of the steps with their feet.

There is also a structural consideration. Steps on cleats that are toward the back side of the stringer provide the stringer with a better top bearing posture. Steps that align with the front edge of the stringer will leave a portion of the stringer head bearing

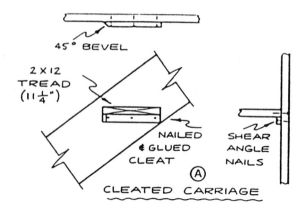

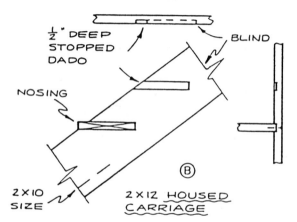

Figure 94 (A) Cleated carriages benefit from having the step toward the rear, (B) dadoed carriages will sustain their compression load best with the step ahead of the uncut portion of the carriage.

unsupported. This is an undersirable condition. It is severe with 2 × 12s and moderate with 2 × 10s, except in cases of maximum unit rise and minimum tread depth (also an undesirable situation).

    The dado method (pronounced "day-doe") is superior to the cleat method since the weight on each cleated step is born on the nails that hold cleats to the carriage. A better system is to dado the carriage to accept the steps. This method requires more time and skill. A dado is a groove cut crosswise of the grain of a board. In the stringer, the dado is at an angle to the edge of the planks. It qualifies as a dado instead of a groove because the annual grain rings in the board are severed. The groove, by comparison, is ploughed out in a direction more or less parallel with the grain.

In cabinet making, dadoes are usually cut halfway through the thickness of the board. Cutting halfway through a $1\frac{1}{2}''$-thick stringer would reduce its strength to that of a $\frac{3}{4}''$ board. A one-third-depth cut ($\frac{1}{2}''$) is enough depth for the step bearing and leaves a stringer that is adequately strong. Builders who do not maintain woodworking shops are not likely to have dado heads (blades) of sufficient capacity to cut a $1\frac{1}{2}''$ dado in a single pass on the radial saw. It is possible to do the operation with smaller dado heads by making two or more passes to plough out the $1\frac{1}{2}''$ dado. In the case of the open stairway, it is assumed that the step to be pocketed in the dado will be dimension stock rather than the more elite milled treads of oak.

A housed freestanding stringer poses different structural considerations when placing the steps across the breadth of the stringer. The stringer is reduced theoretically in strength throughout the portion affected by the cut-out dadoes. The term "theoretically" is used because once the steps are glued and nailed into a snugly fitted joint, the strength is somewhat restored. Nonetheless, a stringer that is dadoed on the front top side will be stronger than one where the blind dadoes are run in from the back underside. Therefore, where steps are installed to the front of the stringers and some auxiliary bearing can be designed to accommodate the head bearing shortcomings, the best of both conditions may be met.

Fastening the steps to the dadoed carriage is accomplished by gluing and end nailing. The success of the holding power is dependent on two elements: the accuracy and tightness of the dado joist and the effectiveness of the nails. Ordinary nails have a tendency to work loose. They are smooth. The vibration from walking on the stairs frequently causes them to work out of the end grain of the step. Resin-coated nails are slightly better. Ring shank nails (annular nails) have the most effective holding power for this purpose. They can be purchased under the name of pole barn nails. A tightly joined step-to-stringer dado joint that is glued and nailed with three 12 or 16d pole barn nails will form a rigid stairway. It will survive many years of use.

A **stop plate** of some sort is needed with a free-flight stair. This stop, sometimes called a kickboard, is needed at the bottom of open stairs to keep the carriages firmly in place. Without a stop plate, the carriages hang from the top end and can be loosened by vibration. There are two simple stop plate designs. A traditional stop is made with a 2 × 4 as long as the width of the stairway. It is fastened to the floor with power nails or concrete anchor bolts. Holes are drilled in the concrete. Vinyl or lead liners are inserted. Lag screws (bolts) are used to hold the 2 × 4 in place. The bottom of the carriages are notched to fit over the 2 × 4 (Fig. 95).

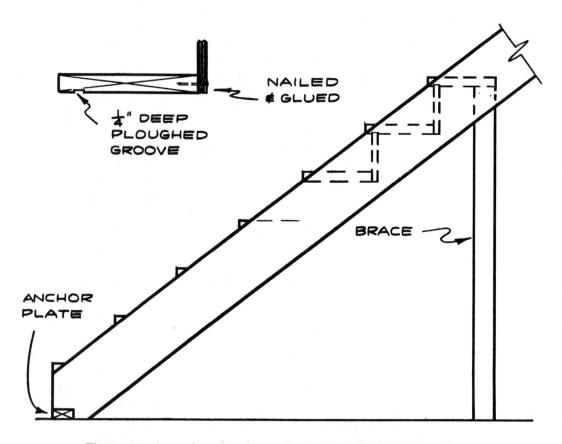

Figure 95 An anchor plate keeps the staircase from sliding out. A knee brace near the center of the carriage cuts the stress in half and nets a solid feeling to the open stair. Risers nailed to the back of the steps eliminate side sway.

Another method of anchoring is to use a short length of angle iron on the inside of each carriage. A piece of $1\frac{1}{2}'' \times 1\frac{1}{2}''$ angle iron, as long as the stringer bearing end, is lag bolted to the concrete floor and cross bolted to the stringer with two carriage bolts in each direction.

A stairway of the design described is limited in width to 3' by most codes since it employs only two stringers. Intermediate support may be provided simply by placing a 2×4 post under each stringer at a point midway up the stringer. With the dadoed design, these posts may be placed against the inside face of the stringers. The upper end bears tightly under a step. Such intermediate support cuts the free span of the stringer in half. It makes it stiffer and capable of carrying heavier loads. It does not, however, improve on the step capacity since that is related only to the span of the step (length across from support to support) and the girth of the step. The intermediate supporting posts will remove any springiness from the stringers. Consequently, a greater sense of strength will be felt. For wider free flights, a third cut type of stringer can be used at the midpoint between the outer stringers.

CUT STRINGER STAIRWAY

The cut stair stringer usually requires the largest plank available, a 2×12, when it is in a free-flight design (no surrounding walls). Triangular pieces are cut out of the carriage stringer at each step location. Each step is made up of two pieces, a tread and a riser. The *tread* is the horizontal step board. The *riser* is a board placed vertically at the back of the step.

The cut stringer loses a lot of its strength from the removal of the cutouts. Most codes mandate that there be no less than $3\frac{1}{2}''$ of solid wood remaining from the point of the cutout to the under edge of the stringer (Fig. 96). In a closed stairwell, this loss of strength is of little concern, as the stringer can be face nailed to each stud along its span. With the free-flight stairway, however, much care must be exercised not to overweaken the stringer with poorly executed cutouts. When the maximum cutout is executed, the $3\frac{1}{2}''$ remaining, in reality, is equivalent to a 2×4.

Some free-flight stairs with cutout stringers have no risers,

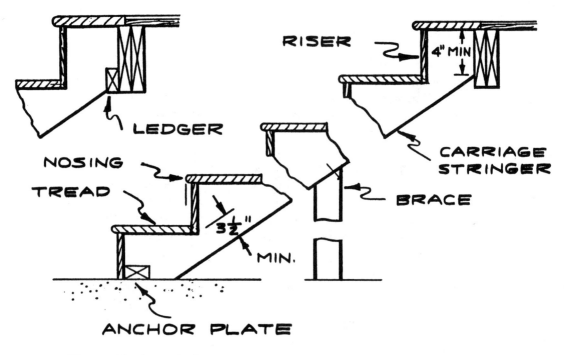

Figure 96 A notched stringer for use as an open stairway will benefit greatly from risers and intermediate support posts, because its effective portion is seldom equivalent to more than a 2 × 4.

as an economy measure. Such a stairway should have intermediate supporting posts without exception. The top of the post will have a pitch cut that matches the slope of the stringer. The post end is carefully pilot drilled and toenailed to the under edge of the stringer. Another suitable technique is to bolt a post to the inside face of each stringer with two carriage bolts.

Risers perform a supporting role to the stringer of a free-flight stairway. The riser should extend downward behind the step. It is then glued and nailed to the back edge of the tread. This formation removes all the potential flexibility of the tread when it is subjected to a concentrated weight (a 200-pound body on one foot). The weight is actually supported by two risers, the one under the front edge of the tread and the one nailed to the back edge. Visualize standing on top of the edge of two boards, totaling a height of about 15" (two risers) and a little over 3' long. It is rigid. Where 13 or 14 of these tread and riser sets are placed into a stringer carriage formation, the resulting stiffness is impressive. Each set is like a large angle iron. The builder who routs out a shallow groove ($\frac{1}{4}$ to $\frac{3}{8}''$) under the front edge of the tread and glues in the top of the riser will produce a stairway unsurpassed in construction quality.

Plywood is the best choice of wood for the riser, although solid wood of $\frac{3}{4}''$ thickness is satisfactory. The multidirectional grain structure of plywood will not split when toe-kicked. A regular board used as a riser will sometimes split when the weight on the back of the step pulls downward on the crosswise running grain.

CLOSED STAIRWAY

The closed stairway is constructed between partitions. It is most commonly found between above ground floors, although partitioned-off basements may also have a closed stairway. The most used carriage stringer design in a stairwell is the cutout type. There are two practical ways of mounting the carriage stringers. They can be nailed directly on the surface of the wall skin (plaster, drywall, or paneling), or they can be nailed on top of an unnotched finish stringer and a 1×4 filler.

The surface-mounting technique calls for the carriage stringers to be nailed on the surface of the wall with nails that anchor in the studs. Because the stringer is usually of a self-supporting design, a single well-placed 16d common nail into each stud is adequate. The nail is placed in the lower $3\frac{1}{2}''$ area of the stringer. Do not nail through the triangular part that holds the tread and riser. This triangular part is vulnerable to splitting off.

A third stringer may be required. If so, it will be centered between the outside stringers. The code maximum width of the stairway with two stringers is 30″ when $\frac{5}{4}$ ($1\frac{1}{16}''$) treads are used. The maximum is 36″ when 2″ ($1\frac{1}{2}''$) dimension treads are used. Therefore, all stairways over 3′ wide will require three stringers. It is rare to find a stairway with only two stringers since the minimum code width is 32″.

During rough construction, the stringers may be temporarily installed as soon as access to the second story is desired. Temporary rough treads are tacked on them so that workers have easy access to the second floor. After the house is closed in and rough plumbed and wired, the stringers may be removed to drywall the partitions in the wall. The stringers are then installed permanently. It should be noted that many framing illustrations show the stringers as though they were mounted directly against the studs. This technique diminishes the bearing space for the treads from $1\frac{1}{2}''$ to an inadequate $\frac{1}{4}''$ after the wall skin and notched finish stringer is added. Installing carriage stringers directly to studs was abandoned when the drywall system took over. Placing the stringers permanently onto bare studs will cause much unnecessary inefficiency. Drywall, or whatever material, will have to be cut around all the notches (a total of 28 notches). Each cut will require some kind of backup between studs to eliminate the flexibility of the wall skin. Beware of the illustration that does not make it clear that carriages and baseboard stringers are both applied on top of the wall skin and not directly to the studs as they were in the days of wet plaster.

After the stringers have been permanently installed on the face of the drywalled stairwell, a nominal $1''$ finish stringer is made for each side of the stairs. This $\frac{3}{4}''$-thick board is a wide piece that serves as a baseboard. It is notched on the lower side in the opposite pattern to the structural stringer before it is installed. The pattern may be traced directly from the carriage. The risers and treads are going to butt snugly against the face of this stringer (Fig. 97). The cutouts on this trim stringer do not have to be precise. The riser is usually $\frac{3}{4}''$ thick and the tread is either $1\frac{1}{16}''$ or $1\frac{1}{2}''$. This allows for some leeway in cutting the trim stringer since the ends of the treads and risers will cover up to the amount of their thickness. The trim stringer is nailed through the wall covering into the studs with finish nails of 8d or 10d size.

A simpler way to fashion a baseboard is to nail a 1×12 board to the wall first (Fig. 98). Nailed directly below this 1×12 is a 1×4 filler. The carriage stringers are then nailed on the surface of these boards. The exposed width of the baseboard needs to be only wide enough to be below the tread contact point

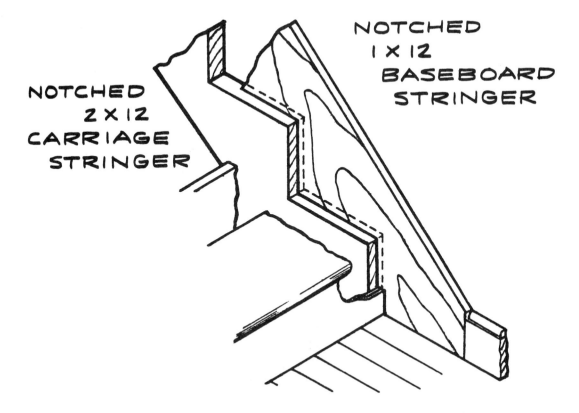

Figure 97 A notched baseboard stringer is fitted to position above the carriage stringer.

and as high above the nosing as desired. This will generally be the same stock width as the stringer or one size smaller. The 1 × 4 filler is nailed to the wall below this trim board. Its lower edge should not protrude below the lower edge of the carriage stringer. To locate this position, the stringer is placed with its head and base bearings in alignment. The underside is then traced on the wall. The carriage is then removed and the 1 × 4 filler is nailed just above the line. The notches of the stringer may also be traced to assure that the trim stringer above is placed correctly to accommodate the risers and treads (parallel to the tread nosings).

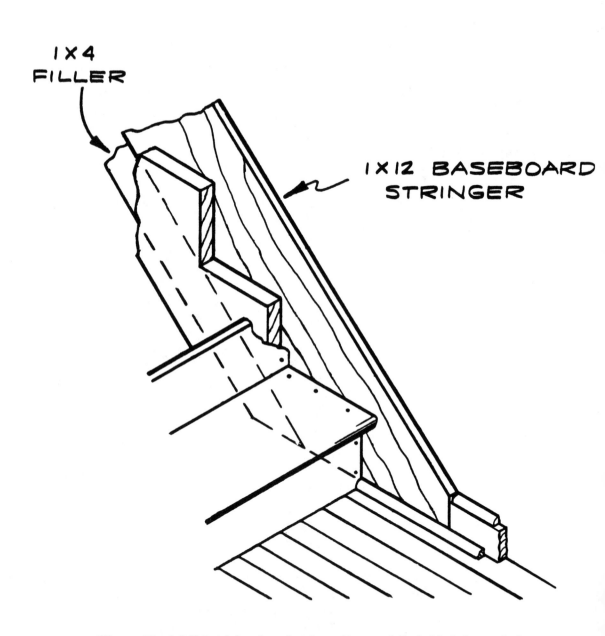

1 X 4
FILLER

1 X 12 BASEBOARD
STRINGER

Figure 98 A full finish baseboard stringer lies partially behind the notched carriage. A filler board is placed below to sustain solid nailing throughout.

150

47 When to Build the Landing

It is not practical to construct temporary landings (platforms), as is done with temporary stairs during rough construction. The platforms are constructed at the time of rough framing as described in an earlier paragraph. After the platforms are in place, each flight of stairs from one level to the next is handled like an independent little stairway. *Reminder*: You must be constantly aware that variable thickness in the surface materials placed on top of the subfloor affects the height of steps and platform landings. It must be taken into account when establishing the position and height of the platform frame and the first and last step cutouts. To maintain equality of step height, it is necessary to add or subtract height for any variable.

The box-framed platform can be constructed against walls that have been covered, but it suffers a basic weakness. Its support will be derived mostly from nails. Where surface mounted, these nails usually bridge across (through) some gypsum to reach the studs. This is a vulnerable weakness unless additional support is provided. Where the cavity underneath the landing is unfinished or closed, this poses no problem. A short 2×4 post is placed under each corner of the box frame. The top of the post is placed in the direction that will cause both adjacent side boards of the box to bear on the top of the vertical 2×4 post.

48 Installing Risers and Treads

After stringers and trim boards are in place, the length of the risers and the ends are custom fitted to each opening. Birch plywood is a favorite material for risers that will be exposed. It is suitable for painting because of its closed-grain surface. It also stains well and blends with oak or maple treads. The high cost of hardwoods makes wall-to-wall carpeting a comparable and attractive alternative to the hardwood staircase. Risers for the carpeted staircase may then be made from an A-C grade of plywood at a considerable saving.

Risers are nailed to the vertical edges of the stringer notches. The stringers ideally will be identical in profile. This is seldom the case. With a three-stringer frame, some adjustment of the tread or riser surfaces is usually necessary (Fig. 99). Use the straight edge of a riser board across the tread-supporting surfaces of the stringers to test. If one tread base of the three is high, trim it down. If one is low, shim it with a strip ripped from the edge of a 2″ board. The step tread should end up resting on all three bearing surfaces and be level. The riser should touch all three vertical edges of the stringers and be square to the walls. These criteria will determine whether to shim or reduce the riser surface.

The top edge of the riser is placed flush with the cutout surfaces of the stringer unless the treads are grooved (Fig. 100). For the grooved tread, the riser will extend above the stringer the exact amount of the groove depth. The bottom edge should rest on the stringers. In this way, the weight on the tread is transferred through the riser to the stringer instead of to the nails that hold the riser on.

Treads are custom fitted in length to each step level. They are surface nailed with finish or casing nails. A hardwood tread will require drill tapping to avoid splitting. The nails at the ends of the tread should be placed no farther than 3/4″ away from the end of the tread. The notched trim stringer above the carriage stringer covers up half the thickness of the bearing surface. The tread is supported by the remaining 3/4″ of surface (Fig. 101). The tap holes must be slanted toward the stringer; otherwise, the nails will miss the stringer and slide down the surface. All nail heads should be set below the surface so that the filler rubbed into the open-grain surface of the oak tread will cover and disguise them. Dimension lumber treads may be nailed with either finishing or full-headed nails. Screwshank flooring nails are good for pulling down warped treads. Concentrate them toward the high points of the tread.

Mounting the stringers on the vertical surface of an unnotched trim board and a filler leaves the full thickness (1½″) of the stringer exposed upon which to mount the treads and risers. This changes the nailing technique. The nails are placed farther back from the ends of the tread. Somewhere between 1 and 1½″ is adequate. A little slant is still needed to make sure that the nail enters the stringer. *Caution*: When driving the nail in this

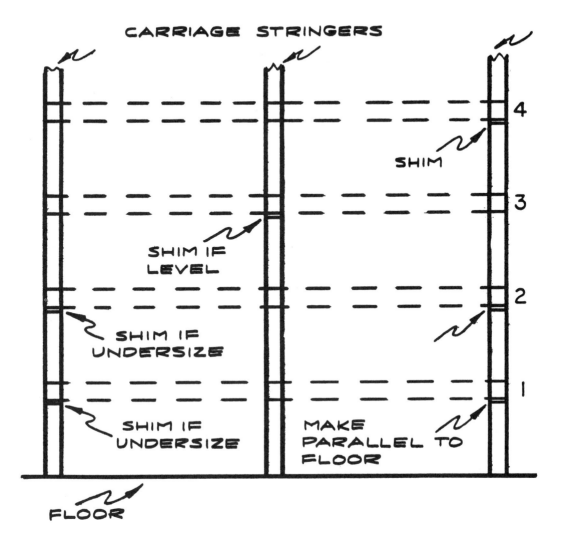

Figure 99 Shown here are four typical misalignment situations. *First step*: Make the tread parallel to the floor; or level by shimming the outside stringer steps, or by cutting down the center step. *Second step*: Check step heights from floor. Determine whether center step is high or side steps are low. Shim-up or cut-down according to correct height and levelness. *Third step*: If the tread is level, then shim the center step. If it is unlevel, cut down the step on the high side. Compare with height from the floor. *Fourth step*: If the tread checks level, shim the low step. If the tread checks high over the step that it does not touch, then cut down the center step.

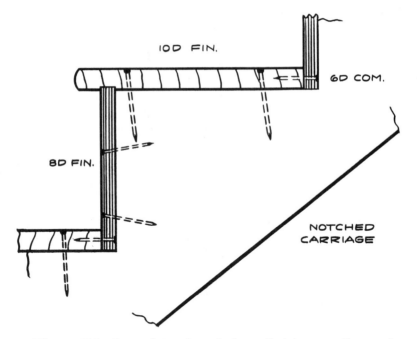

Figure 100 Grooved treads and risers that bear on the carriage step will net a sturdy staircase.

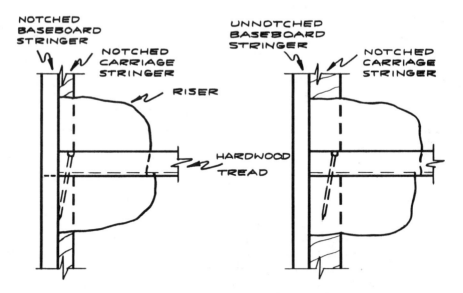

Figure 101 The step tread will bear on only ³/₄″ where a notched baseboard stringer is used. The full stringer lapped by a notched carriage provides 1½″ of bearing for the tread. In both cases, a pilot hole should be drilled for each hole and should be slanted toward the thickest body of the carriage step.

area, it is exceptionally easy to damage the finish stringer surface with hammer dents. A sheet metal shield is an excellent
preventive tool to have on hand. Hold it in position to cover the
face of the trim board while hammering in the nails.

49 Design and Construction Rules

Many a stairway has been made by trial and error. There is no
need to subject oneself to such a task, a potential ordeal, when
the use of a few rules and formulas will make a product of near
perfection possible. It makes sense to know the rules and principles before attempting a layout on either a working drawing or a
carriage plank.

The following rules from the Federal Housing Administration Minimum Property Standards (FHA MPS), Southern Building Code Congress International (SBCCI), and others apply.

1. **The minimum effective depth** of a cut stringer is $3\frac{1}{2}''$
    (the lower side of the stringer) perpendicular to the rake.

2. **The top bearing** end of the stringer (the vertical edge)
    shall not be less than $4''$ unless otherwise adequately
    anchored.

3. **A center stringer** is required when the distance between
    the outside stringers is greater than $30''$ for $1\frac{1}{16}''$ treads
    or $36''$ for $1\frac{1}{2}''$ treads.

4. **Headroom** should not be less than $6'\text{-}8''$ measured verti-
    cally from an imaginary line intersecting all nosing ex-
    tremities to the lowest obstruction above.

5. **Open stairs** shall have an anchoring system at the bot-
    tom.

6. **Winders** shall meet the common tread depth not farther
    than $18''$ from the hub of their acute angle (Fig. 102a).

7. **A landing** at the foot of a stair run shall not be less than
    $30''$ deep ahead of the tread nosing (Fig. 102b). The step
    rise should not be less than $7''$ or greater than $8''$.

8. **The tread run** (the horizontal cutout on the carriage)
    should not be less than $9''$.

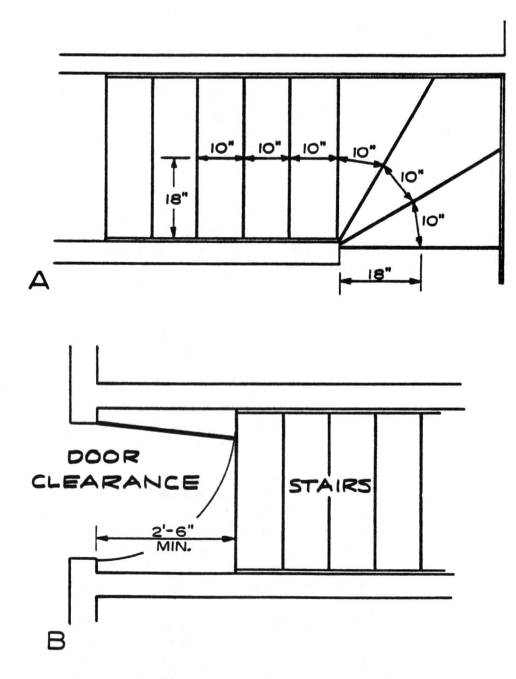

Figure 102 (A) Winders must have at least a full depth tread at a point within 18″ of the small end of the tread, (B) the minimum depth of a landing is 30″ or whatever the door width is if it is wider than 30″.

156

9. **The tread** should not be less than $10\frac{1}{8}''$.
10. **The nosing** should not be less than $1\frac{1}{8}''$ or greater than the tread thickness.

The following principles also apply:

1. The sum of the unit rise and run should equal $17''$ or the sum of two rises and one run should equal $25''$.
2. The overall run of a stringer *does not* include the head bearing end of the stringer.

Ignoring this last bit of knowledge has probably been the greatest cause of ill-designed and constructed stairways where detail plans were not available or not correctly interpreted. With these basic rules and principles, the reader is now ready to attempt the computation required to draw a dimensioned profile and to lay out the stringer on a plank (also see Fig. 96).

50 Predesigned or Custom-Designed Stairs

There are two ways to go about designing stairs. One way is to design the carriage first. The length of the rough opening in the floor is then established from the section view. It is transposed to the floor plan. On the floor plan, enough length must be provided to accommodate the total run of the stringer. The *total run* of the stringer is the sum of the units of run. The *overall* run of the stringer includes the horizontal top of the head bearing part of the carriage, which is covered with flooring. Another variable exists with open stairs leading to a basement. A portion of *one* step at the bottom can fall under the ceiling (the first floor). (See Fig. 107.) There will still be adequate headroom. These two design conditions make it possible to have a rough opening in the floor that is approximately one-half unit run shorter than the overall run. When the stairway is designed before the floor plan is completed, a section drawing is made to scale (the larger, the better). The factor that will control the minimum possible rough-

opening length will be the headroom. *Headroom* may be defined
as the vertical distance from a line connecting the nosings of the
treads to the lowest obstruction above. *Head clearance* is another
term for this distance. It will be noted that this minimum height
of 6'-8" conforms with the standard door height most commonly
found in a residence.

The second and more common method of designing a stairway is to allow a recognized minimum space or more for the
stairway on a floor plan. A stair detail plan may not always be
furnished. It then becomes the builder's job to figure out the
layout (Fig. 103). A rule of thumb for the length of a rough
opening in the first floor leading to a basement is a minimum of
9'-6". A second-floor opening should not be less than 10' according to this rule of thumb. These lengths are true in essence, but
they do not include the distance required for the bearing head of
the carriage. Six to eight inches must be added to the floor plan
opening to establish the rough opening.

A significant error is frequently caused by misinterpretation
of the floor plan. On the plan a line is seen that represents a
change of levels. This line is the edge of the nosing on the floor
level. It does *not* represent the location of the joist header in the
rough floor (Fig 104). The header will be about 6 to 8" back from
this plan line. On those occasions when a header is incorrectly
placed at this nosing line, the intended total run of the stringer
will be shortened by as much as one unit of run. This will cause
a stringer to be made with higher rises and a steeper, less desirable pitch. This also affects the headroom by shortening it. This
problem may cause an inspection failure. The builder may be
required to tear out and redo—a costly remedial situation. Few
of the parts can be reused. Only the risers can be cut down to
size. The treads will be too narrow. The stringers are a total loss.

Another error frequently occurs at this point. Assume that
the builder followed a good detail plan and placed the floor
header in the correct location. The intended stairway leads to a
basement. As is the logical custom, the concrete basement floor
will not be poured until the roof is completed. Therefore, the stair
stringers will be one of the last framing details. In the meantime,
the first floor will probably be sheathed with plywood. The
sheather forgets to allow the sheathing to extend beyond the

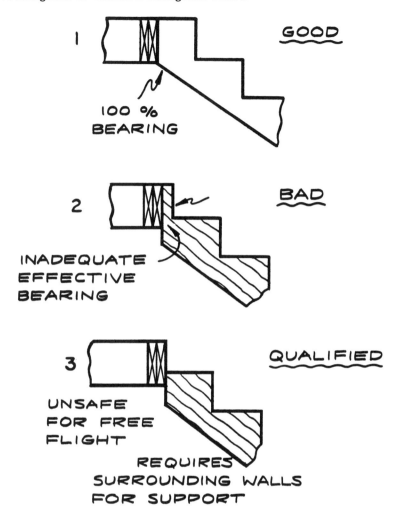

Figure 103 *Drawing 1* shows an ideal head bearing posture where all the end of the carriage stringer is leaning on the headers. *Drawing 2* is a poor design for any circumstance. *Drawing 3* is a poor design for a free flight stair, but would be tolerable for a stairwell where the carriages can be nailed to the studs of the well partitions.

headers into the opening. It should extend to the point where the first riser will be. By ignoring or forgetting this, a valuable tie is lost. The uninterrupted sheathing at this location should form an effective tie from the floor frame onto the top head of the stringer

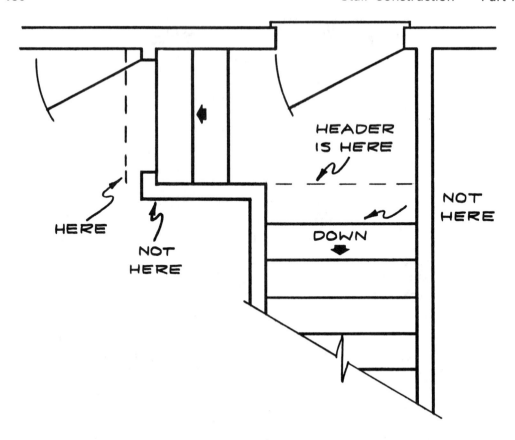

Figure 104 The line on a floor plan indicates where a step changes levels (the edge of the nosing on the landing or floor). The header should be at least 8″ farther back as the floor runs out on top the head of the carriage.

(Fig. 105). An effective method of assuring this sheathing tie is to let it hang beyond the header 10 to 12″. At this stage it is not known where the precise drop-off point will be. By leaving this excess sheathing, it is possible to cut it precisely after the stringer is installed. Usually, the whole plywood sheet can be left intact and the cut made later.

Let us assume that the architect or designer follows the latter technique, floor plan first, stair detail second. Some limitations are now imposed on the design. The stairway incline is confined to a cubical well of certain dimensions that cannot be

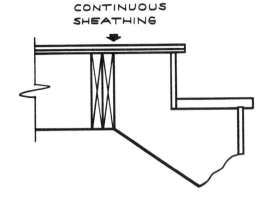

CONTINUOUS
SHEATHING

Figure 105 Permit sheathing and underlayment to extend beyond the header 10″ or more. Cut it off to form a standard nosing after the stair carriages are permanently installed. Do not cut it off at the header, which would destroy its tying function.

altered without changing the floor plan. The total run is confined to the horizontal length of the opening. The total rise is a fixed amount of distance. The project is now one of customizing the stairway profile to these dimensional limits.

TOTAL RISE

Total rise is the distance vertically from one floor surface to another for which the stairway is to be designed. It does not matter whether the stairway is curved, straight, or one of the turning designs. The sum of the unit levels in the stairway is the total rise. The dimension to use for the total rise number is the *actual* height that exists. A designer or carpenter should never scale a drawing to get this number. It must be derived by mathematics and by actual measurement. The individual components are assessed for their actual size. Take two examples, a typical basement height and a first floor-to-second floor height.

A typical block wall basement will contain 12 blocks of height. The unit block height (laid measure) is 8″. Twelve blocks net a total height of 96″. A 4″ concrete floor is poured on top of the footing where the blocks sit, so 4″ is subtracted from the 96″, leaving 92″ of block wall exposed above the floor. A wood sill rests on top of the wall, which adds 1½″ of height. Fiberglass sill sealer is completely compressible, so it adds no height. The box floor has 2 × 10 joists and headers, so 9¼″ of height is added.

The subfloor is ½" plywood, and the underlayment flooring is ⅝" particle board. The problem is

$$92 + 1\tfrac{1}{2} + 9\tfrac{1}{4} + \tfrac{1}{2} + \tfrac{5}{8} = 103\ \tfrac{7}{8}''$$

For practical purposes this figure could be rounded to 104". This is a theoretical addition of materials to be used for drawing purposes. On the site, *the height should be measured and taken exactly as it exists for the purpose of laying out the stringer.*

From first to second floor, a typical total rise will accumulate the following addition. The ⅝" particle board underlayment is conventionally laid on top of the subfloor, as are the partition soles (the open-building technique is an exception). Where the stringer rests on the subfloor, the particle board reduces the room height by ⅝". For our sample problem this can be subtracted immediately from the sole height ($1\tfrac{1}{2} - \tfrac{5}{8} = \tfrac{7}{8}''$ of sole height above the finish floor level). There remains the following quantities to add: ⅞" of exposed sole, a precut stud of 92⅝", a double plate ($1\tfrac{1}{2}'' + 1\tfrac{1}{2}''$) of 3" and a ceiling/floor joist of 9¼", a ½" subfloor, and a ⅝" underlayment on the second floor. The problem is

$$\tfrac{7}{8} + 92\tfrac{5}{8} + 3 + 9\tfrac{1}{4} + \tfrac{1}{2} + \tfrac{5}{8} = 106\ \tfrac{7}{8}''$$

On a calculator, the problem looks like this

$$.875 + 92.625 + 3 + 9.25 + .5 + .625 = 106.875''$$

The sum will vary according to the material sizes. For example, 2 × 8 joists will reduce the figure by 2" to 104.875". On the site, the actual height should be found, but be careful to add materials that are not yet installed, such as flooring.

NUMBER OF RISERS

Most basement stairways will have 13 or 14 steps (units of rise). The construction of the foundation wall affects the height, which in turn affects the quantity of steps that will qualify under the minimum–maximum rule. The first floor-to-second floor stairway, where precut studs are used, will usually have 14 units of rise.

Apply these unit-rise modules to the basement example. Try the number 13 first.

$$104'' \div 13 = 8'' \text{ actual rise}$$

This is an acceptable unit rise, although it is at the top of the maximum range. It is the steepest incline considered practical. The next full quantity of rise units to produce a shorter unit of rise is 14. Divided by 14, the 104" nets a unit rise of 7.4285714" (by calculator). Reduced to a fraction of an inch, it comes out just under 7 $7/16$". This is a more comfortable step when climbing. It requires a little more total run to maintain the headroom desired. In most cases, this will cause a small loss in floor space. Such a loss is well worth it in terms of the added relief, the climbing comfort, over a period of years.

The total rise in the first-to-second floor example was 106$7/8$". Fourteen units of rise creates the following problem:

$$106 \, 7/8 \div 14 = 7.6339285$$

The fractional inch, 0.6339285 transposes to 20.29 thirty-seconds or slightly over $5/8$". Therefore, the unit rise dimension that can be used in the layout process is 7$5/8$". When using a calculator, the fractional-inch remainder can be multiplied by 32 first to see if you can find the rise to the closest $1/32$". This can be rounded to the closest $1/16$" when it falls within the upper or lower quadrant of the whole decimal (upper or lower 25%). When it falls in the middle two quadrants (0.25 to 0.75), it should be left in thirty-seconds of an inch. Decimal fractions, in this midrange, are closer to the nearest thirty-second than to the nearest sixteenth. When dividing a stringer into equal units of rise, working to a $1/32$" tolerance is quite possible and practical for the good carpenter who keeps his pencil sharp for the layout.

RUN UNIT DEPTH

The quantity of treads (run units) is always one less than the quantity of risers. This is because the stringer starts with and ends with a riser. The last step, so to speak, is the floor, both at the bottom and the top (see Fig. 88).

The unit run, according to the rules, may be as much as 1$1/2$" less than the tread depth since 1$1/2$" is the maximum overhang of the nosing with dimension lumber treads (Fig. 106). A stringer notch can be designed to accommodate a dimension lumber tread precisely so that the tread can be used without ripping. For example, any run variation between 9¾″ and 10⅛″ will accept a 2 × 12 tread (11¼″). On the 9¾″ run, the tread will hang over the maximum 1½″. On the 10⅛″ run, the 11¼″ tread will hang over the minimum amount, 1⅛″. Therefore, all units of run that fall between 9¾″ and 10⅛″ may be fitted with stock 2 × 12s without machining. Units that fall between 9″ (the minimum) and 9¾″ (the minimum for stock 2 × 12) must be custom ripped. For maximum nosing (1½″ with dimension stock), the tread will be 1½″ plus the unit run dimension.

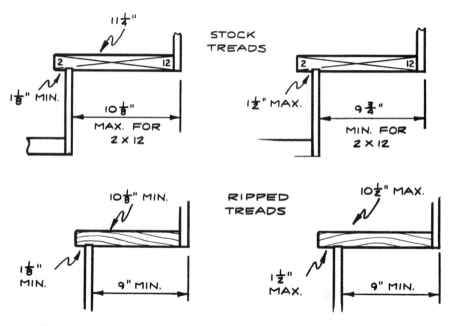

Figure 106 Stock 2 × 12s may be used without customizing where the unit run range falls within 9¾ to 10 ⅛″. From the minimum unit run of 9 to 9¾″ the 2 × 12s will have to be ripped to a size 1½″ wider than the run figure.

A Typical Unit Run Problem. A typical run situation is as follows. The designer has provided 10′ of length on the floor plan in accordance with the minimum rule of thumb. The 120″ is divided by 13 to net a 9.23″ unit run. The .23 fraction may be rounded to .25 (¼″). This unit of run is smaller than is acceptable for the stock 2 × 12 range. Therefore, the treads will need to be custom ripped to 10¾″. By adding the maximum nosing (1½″) to the unit run (9¼″), the deepest tread possible is 10¾″ for this stairway.

This example makes the assumption that the face of the bottom riser will be directly below the floor opening above. In this position, the head clearance will be the room height minus one unit of rise. In the 12-block basement example, the room height is 93½″, 12 blocks (96″) minus a 4″ concrete floor plus a 1½″ sill. Subtracting the 7 7/16″ bottom step from the 14-riser example, the headroom is 86¹/₁₆″ (Fig. 107). This is a case where the step could be extended out under the opening above a few inches without compromising the headroom. It could extend to a

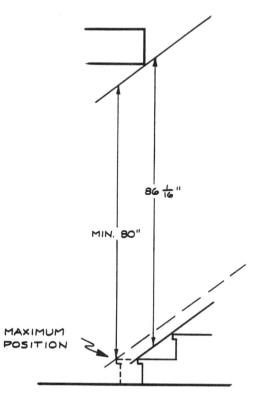

Figure 107 Where the unit run of a stringer is limited by a minimum-sized stairwell opening, the lower step can be run ahead of the obstruction above to a point where the headroom line indicates the minimum 6′-8″ point.

point where the nosing pitch line measured 6'-8" to the opening above. It is also an example of the nontechnical approach to stairwell design. Had the stairway been laid out to scale on a drawing first, it would have been found that an opening a few inches longer would make it possible to use treads of full 2 × 12 stock. The run units would need to be designed at a minimum of 9¾". Thirteen of these units would make a floor opening of 126 ¾" (10'-6 ¾"). This design will produce the maximum nosing. It then comes down to a question of expending a little more floor space above to maintain better headroom or lengthening out the stringer to attain deeper treads at the cost of minimum headroom.

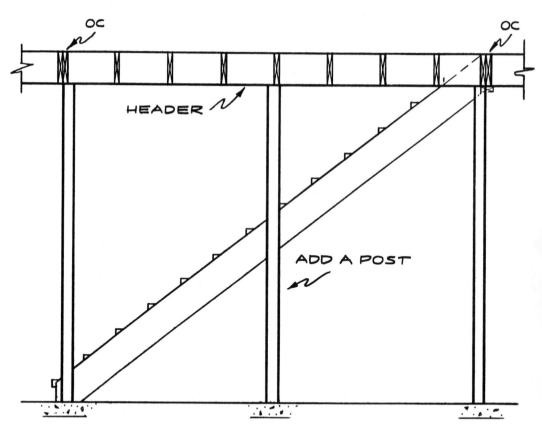

Figure 108 A stairwell header on the long side which is over 10' long may be supported adequately by adding another post at the center of the span.

From this exercise it can be seen that a little mathematics can make it possible to know the floor opening length that will be needed when you want to use full 2 × 12 treads. It also makes it clear that the two rule-of-thumb figures (9'-6" and 10') for rough openings are not only deceptive but limiting. All treads will be less than 11¼" deep with these openings. The origin of the 10' rule may have sprung from the FHA rule that a double header perpendicular to the floor joist that forms a side of the stairwell may not exceed 10' in length. This points out the fact that a partition wall under those joist tails is a superior method of supporting them. The header in excess of 10', on the other hand, can simply be supported by a third post at the center, making a total of three (Fig. 108). The center post will also double as a support for the carriage.

51 Laying out the Carriage Stringer

For years the conventional method of laying out a stringer has been to step off the notches with a framing square. The method is *not* as accurate as it could be. It is plagued with the short-measuring-instrument characteristic. It has more potential for inaccuracy than exists when a room length is measured with a ruler instead of a tape measure. The Appendix contains a table of hypotenuse moduli that will make it possible to lay out a stringer more accurately.

STEP-OFF METHOD

To practice the traditional step-off technique, the framing square is placed on the stringer. The rise is traced along the tongue (the 16" side) and the run is traced along the edge of the body (the 24" side). The tracing must be done on both outside or both inside edges of the square throughout the task (Fig. 109). The rise and run figures are located on the square and held flush with the top

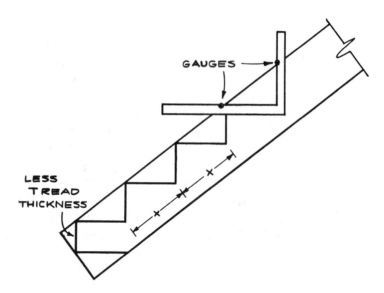

Figure 109 "Stepping off" the carriage pattern is more accurate when gauges are used on the framing square, and the hypotenuse are constantly monitored for equality.

edge of the stringer. The square is then moved ahead to the next cutout and traced again. This is repeated as many times as there are cutouts. The accuracy of the step-off technique suffers from the multiple movement and the short-measuring-tool syndrome. The edges of dimension stock are rounded. It is difficult to set the square down precisely over the last mark looking down on a rounded edge. Second, it is difficult to line up two sets of locations and figures and trace along two edges without permitting any movement in the square. These inaccuracies can be partially eliminated by using a pair of clamp-on gauges. These gauges are useful for rafter layout, stair stringers, and any other place where uniform angles are desired. With one placed on the rise mark and one on the run mark, the square will return to the identical angles each time it is moved along the plank. This leaves only the task of lining up the lower gauge mark over the previous rise line. With practice, the position of one's head and the angle of the vision will become more consistent. A fairly accurate set of tracings will result.

Proof testing the layouts is done easily by measuring between the points of the cutout tracings. These hypotenuse of each of the triangles must be identical to the others to produce uniform steps. To check the accuracy of run and rise depth (distance from the point to the under edge of the stringer), a measurement is taken at right angles from the underedge of the stringer to the point. It will be found that without gauges on the square the accuracy and uniformity will not be good. With gauges it is improved. The accuracy can be made as perfect as the thickness of a pencil line when gauges are used in conjunction with the hypotenuse table.

CROOKED BOARD PROBLEM

To understand why it is difficult to plot perfect cutouts, it is necessary to comprehend the nature of lumber. The perfectly straight 2 × 12 plank in the length needed is a rarity. Some accommodating lumberyards will allow you to pick through a pile until you find two or three that appear to be suitable. Even so, by the time they are transported to the site under the rays of the hot sun or perhaps get soaked in a rain shower, the shape begins to change. One of the quickest and most certain ways to alter the shape of a board is to lay it flat on the ground for a few hours.

Visualize an extremely crooked plank with cutouts traced on it. It is readily seen that the hypotenuse line parallels the curve of the edge of the board. In this configuration, none of the run lines are parallel to each other and none of the rise lines are parallel to each other. When the stringer is plotted with the crown up, the hypotenuse units are longer than natural. If the cutouts are plotted on the concave edge, each hypotenuse will be shorter. In neither position, crown up or crown down, is a crooked board a good choice for a stringer. To produce level steps and plumb risers, it is necessary to have a straightedge as a guide by which to lay out the step.

STRINGER LAYOUT ON A STRAIGHT BOARD

Let us assume that three straight boards have been acquired. If not, let us conclude that three can be machined to a point where the crowned edge is now straight. To have uniformly wide boards, each of the two or three will have to be ripped parallel using the narrowest dimension as the standard. Let us use the hypotenuse table for a uniform 10″ run unit (see the Appendix).

1. Place one gauge on the outside edge of the body of the framing square at the 10″ mark. Place the other gauge on the outside of the tongue at the place that will net your exact unit of rise. Place the square on the surface of the plank with the gauges touching. Adjust the gauges if necessary until the rise and run lengths measure correctly from the edge of the carriage to the point of the square.
2. Place the square on the surface of the board with the gauges touching the top edge (Fig. 110). Place it close

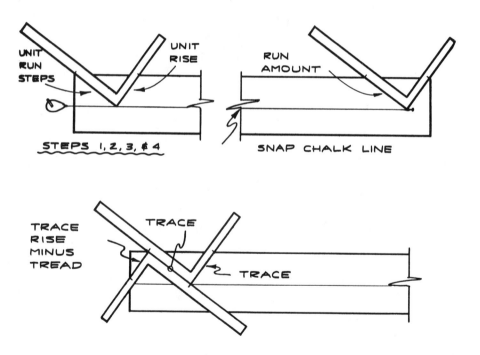

Figure 110 The first four steps toward laying out a carriage stringer involve accurately locating and marking the hypotenuse line, which will pass through all the junctions between each step and rise.

to the bottom end of the stringer. Make a sharp pencil dot at the corner of the square.

3. Move the square to the other end of the board and make a dot at the point of the square.

4. Draw a chalk line tightly the full length of the board and passing over the two dots. Snap it. When working alone, place a small nail in one dot to hold the end of your chalk line. This line is the hypotenuse behind (below) all the step triangles.

5. Locate the first rise mark at the bottom. Only the first rise will be reduced by an amount equal to the tread thickness. Place the square with gauges in the approximate location. Place a second square under it with the bodies back to back. The tongue of the lower square will be in a position to trace the first rise (pointing down). The gauge square is in position to trace the first run and the second rise (tongue pointing up). Slide the assembly down the board until the rise figure, minus the tread thickness, is at the lower end of the board, the corner on the underedge. Trace along the vertical edge of the tongue of the lower square. This is the first rise mark.

6. Take away the lower square without moving the upper square. Trace along the lower edge of the body on the gauge square. This is the first run step. Trace along the outer edge of the tongue. This is the second rise line.

7. Make a base line parallel to the first step starting at the bottom point of the first rise at the end of the board (Fig. 111). Lay out the profile of the kickboard.

8. Find the hypotenuse figure on the table in the Appendix that corresponds to your rise and run combination. Starting at the point of the first cutout, mark off the figures along the chalk line as many times as there are cutouts. Indent the position with a nail point and circle it with a pencil.

9. Move the square gauge up the stringer to the second point. Place the corner of the square precisely on the hypotenuse point. Trace the rise and run lines along the edges of the square. Move along to each succeeding mark and trace.

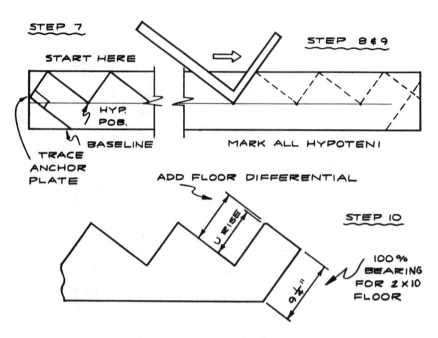

Figure 111 The bottom bearing of the stringer is laid out parallel to the bottom step. Trace the kickplate cutout. Mark and indent all the hypotenuse points on the chalk line. Place the point of the square on each indentation and trace all the remaining profiles. Plot the top rise line and the bearing head line.

10. The last level mark will be the one where the top of the stringer meets the underside of the flooring. The stringer board may not be long enough for the tongue gauge to rest on the edge out beyond this point. Remove the gauges from the square. Place the tongue of the square alongside the last rise line pointing down. The blade is pointing to the underedge of the stringer. The height figure on the tongue is aligned with the last tread line. This height may be different from that of rises. When the tread thickness is thicker than the combination of floor materials, the last rise will be greater by the amount of difference. The height is the unit rise from the upper floor level minus the total floor thickness. Trace all the way across the stringer on the

top of the blade. *Example*: When 1½″ treads are being used on steps below but the sheathing and underlayment floor comprise the topping of the stringer, a discrepancy will exist. Assuming that the floor sheathing is ½″ thick and the particle board is ⅝″, the sum will be 1⅛″. The ⅜″ difference will be made up with the top rise unit of the stringer in order to reach the underside of the flooring. The point of the square will protrude a little beyond the front edge of the stringer. The resulting absence of this little point of wood on the last step is of no consequence, as the riser supports the front edge of the tread.

11. Locate the head bearing. Place the square with the outer edge of the body along the top level line. The tongue will be pointing down and on the underside of the stringer. Move the square right or left until the figure on the tongue that is the same as the actual size of your floor joist header is in line with the underedge of the stringer. Trace a plumb line along the tongue. This will produce a head on the stringer that bears 100% on the header, an ideal bearing.

CUTTING THE STRINGER

Cut out the stringer very carefully (Fig. 112). Cut only in the scrap wood, leaving the pencil lines intact. *Do not cut beyond the point of the cutout.* The circular saw may be used for most of each cut, but the cut will have to be completed with a straight saw, either hand or power.

After completing one stringer, it may be used as a template. Whether you choose to use it or not will depend on how accurate it appears to be. The accuracy can be proofed to a certain extent by placing the framing square into each completed cutout and checking the squareness and the rise and run figures. The variance between cutouts can be checked across the outer points. This distance should be the same as used on the hypotenuse chalk line under the cutouts.

Should the proofing show inaccuracies to any degree, it will

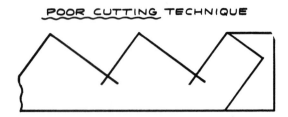

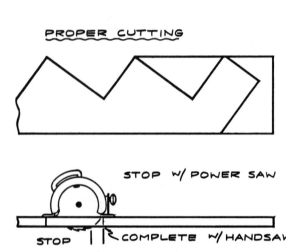

Figure 112 Do not weaken a stair stringer by over running the saw cuts. Complete the power cuts with a handsaw, holding the blade perpendicular.

be best to lay out the remaining stringers independently. After they are laid out, the first stringer can be placed on top of the layout. This will produce an overall picture of the problem and suggest where it can be improved.

After all three stringers have been cut, clamp them side by side with the bottoms and tops perfectly flush. Inaccurate lineup of run levels and rise surfaces may be rectified to a certain extent by trimming. Caution and judgment are needed. Like shortening table legs, too much trimming may defeat the project.

CHOOSING A UNIT OF RUN

Each table has been made for a specific unit run. The unit run is controllable by design. Any figure from 9 to 10$\frac{1}{8}$" may serve. The

2 × 12 dimension tread is the largest stock tread available. It is practical on unit runs from 9³/₄ to 10¹/₈″. This depth of run nets nosing overhang variables from the 1¹/₂″ maximum to the 1¹/₈″ minimum depth nosing.

These variables provide the floor plan designer with some latitude in choosing the total run. He or she can pick a unit run size and tread combination and multiply the run units by the quantity of steps to find a total run. The total run is then worked into the floor plan. Remember that there is one less step than rise. For example, if the choice is for 14 risers, then multiply the desired unit run by 13. Let us say that a full 11¹/₄″ unripped tread and a maximum 1¹/₂″ nosing are desired. The run unit will be 9³/₄″.

$$13 \times 9.75 = 126.75 \quad \text{or} \quad 10'\text{-}6^3/_4''$$

Since the bottom step can run out under the ceiling a few inches before contacting the minimum height line that touches the nosings, it will be safe to allow a space on the floor plan of about 10′-6″ plus or minus an inch or two. This rule-of-thumb designing technique assumes a basement wall height comprised of 12 block units (96″) minus a 4″ concrete floor. Should the designer be cramped for total run space, the sacrifice can be made by shortening the run units and ripping the treads to a depth that does not exceed 1¹/₂″ more than the unit run.

Choosing the unit rise does not present as many options. The total rise is a fixed design dimension. The height is derived from the size of the materials that are combined. There are usually no more than two choices when divided by a number that will result in a suitable rise (7 to 8″). It is then only a choice of a higher unit rise combined with a shorter run or a lower unit rise combined with a longer total run and deeper treads.

READING THE HYPOTENUSE TABLE

The tables presented in the Appendix cover the range of run units in ¹/₈″ modules for uncut 2 × 12s and 2 × 10s. For any run figure between these modules, the builder/designer can easily work out his or her own hypotenuse by substituting the actual figure into the Pythagorean theorem,

$$a^2 \; + \; b^2 \; = \; c^2$$

The first step is to *establish the exact unit rise and run dimensions* that apply. This is accomplished by measuring the actual length of the opening in the floor and the actual height from one floor level to the next. Remember to add thickness for materials that are not yet on the top floor or subtract for materials that are not yet on the bottom floor. Also remember to allow several horizontal inches (approximately 6″) for the head bearing that projects out from the floor joist header.

Find the table of uniform run units that matches your unit of run or that is slightly less. Taking a higher run will decrease headroom. Where your plan permits the bottom step to extend beyond the headroom point, a slightly larger unit-of-run table can be used. Find the horizontal line in which your rise number appears in the left vertical column. Choose the one that is the closest in whole sixteenths of an inch. Move across this line to the right vertical column. Here you will find the hypotenuse of each step triangle. If your rise number is an uneven fraction, it should be interpreted to the $\frac{1}{32}$″. This number is then matched to the closest thirty-second on the table, or a hypotenuse figure can be chosen that is between the two that are above and below your rise number. For example, if your rise turns out to be 7 $\frac{13}{32}$″, the $\frac{13}{32}$ is between $\frac{3}{8}$ ($\frac{12}{32}$) and $\frac{7}{16}$ ($\frac{14}{32}$), so the hypotenuse will be between these two lines on the table. This would seem to be splitting hairs when it comes to cutting out notches with a saw that may remove a $\frac{1}{8}$″ kerf. It is significant, however, when laying out with the step-off method. Fourteen risers with a $\frac{1}{16}$″ error in height can result in $\frac{7}{8}$″ of error in the total rise. The result will be a carriage with steps that slope toward the nosing or slope toward the riser, depending on whether the error was oversize or undersize.

The tables that appear in the Appendix span a unit rise range of 7 to 8″ and a unit run range from 9 to 10″. The rise numbers are computed to the nearest $\frac{1}{16}$″. If a small error occurs in total rise, the unit hypotenuse may be lengthened out or shortened a small part of a thirty-second to compensate. For this type of accuracy, a very sharp round lead, hard lead pencil, or a prick punch will do a better job than a flat carpenter pencil. A 5H to 8H drawing pencil of the drafting type will work well.

For those who enjoy and feel competent with the calculator or computer, the problems may be worked with decimals and related to the inches on the framing square that are divided in tenths.

52 FHA Minimum Standards

The Federal Housing Administration Minimum Property Standards (Table 1) are constantly being revised. These requirements constitute reasonable minimums to adhere to, whether or not the house comes under FHA jurisdiction. There is only one minimum with which the author would take issue. That is the 6'-4" head-

TABLE 1   STAIRWAY DESIGN

	Private exterior stairs (attached to dwelling)		Private and common[a] interior stairs	
	Entrance	Basement	Main	Basement
Minimum clear headroom	—	—	6'-8"	6'-4"
Minimum width[b]	2'-8"	2'-8"	2'-8"	2'-8"
Minimum tread[c]	11"	11"	9"	9"
Minimum nosing	—	—	d	d
Maximum riser[c,e]	7½"	7½"	8¼"	8¼"
Winders[e,f]	Run at point 18" from converging end shall not be less than straight portion.			

[a] Stairway serving two living units.

[b] Clear of handrail.

[c] All treads shall be the same width and all risers the same height in a flight of stairs.

[d] Closed riser, 1⅛" nosing; open riser, ½" nosing.

[e] Winders are not permitted in common stairs.

[f] In a building required to be accessible to the physically handicapped, the maximum riser is 7½". Winders or open risers shall not be used in such buildings. The width of a landing shall be not less than the width of the stairs, and its depth shall be not less than 2'-6". The swing of a door opening on a stairway shall not overlap the top step.

room for a basement stairway. Many people in the United States find this height to be oppressive. A common disability that goes along with the over-six-footer is back trouble. The builder who builds to sell will limit prospects with this low-clearance stairwell. The owner who builds to live in the house may suffer years of aggravation. If he or she attempts to solve the problem by selling, the owner may have to wait for a customer whose height does not pose a problem in the short stairwell. It seems logical to stick with the door height standard of 6'-8" as a minimum head clearance for any stairway that will have frequent use.

REVIEW TOPICS

1. Sketch and label a single-line plan view of each of the following stair types: (a) straight run, (b) L shape with one landing platform, (c) switchback, (d) U (double L) with two landing platforms, (e) L with winders.
2. Explain what a freestanding or open stairway is.
3. Compare and discuss the comparative merits and faults of a cleated and a dadoed stair stringer design.
4. Of the three carriage stringer designs for a free-flight stairway to a basement, which requires knee braces the most? Explain why.
5. Describe fully the penalties that will be paid if stair carriages are permanently nailed to bare studding and the staircase is then completed.
6. Where three notched carriage stringers are required, the slightest difference in step height will cause the tread to bear only on two steps. Analyze the various situations and describe how to go about correcting each so that each tread will bear equally on all three steps.
7. Describe the technique of fastening the ends of hardwood treads to a carriage under a notched baseboard stringer and to a carriage on the surface of an unnotched baseboard stringer.
8. Explain why so many stairways are altered in a detrimental way due to incorrect floor plan interpretation. Tell how this can be avoided.
9. Explain the faults incurred with the step-off method of laying out stringer steps.
10. Describe each step in order using the hypotenuse table in the Appendix

that will lead to a successful layout of stair carriage stringers. Remember to clarify the differences between the bottom and top steps and the common steps between.

11. Describe the technique and care that should be taken when cutting the notches in a stair stringer.

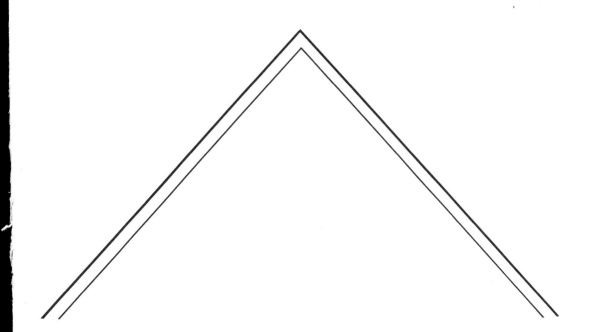

Appendix

STAIR STRINGER HYPOTENUSE TABLE FOR A *9″* UNIT RUN: $a^2 + b^2 = c^2$.

Rise in fractions (*a*)	Rise in decimals (*a*)	Square of the rise (a^2)		Square of the run (b^2)	Unit hypotenuse (*c*) Decimals	Fractions
7	7	49.	+	81.	11.40	$11^{13}/_{32}$
$7^1/_{16}$	7.0625	49.88	+	81.	11.44	$11^7/_{16}$
$7^1/_8$	7.125	50.77	+	81.	11.48	$11^{15}/_{32}$
$7^3/_{16}$	7.1875	51.66	+	81.	11.52	$11^1/_2$
$7^1/_4$	7.25	52.56	+	81.	11.56	$11^9/_{16}$
$7^5/_{16}$	7.3125	53.47	+	81.	11.60	$11^{19}/_{32}$
$7^3/_8$	7.375	54.39	+	81.	11.64	$11^5/_8$
$7^7/_{16}$	7.4375	55.32	+	81.	11.68	$11^{11}/_{16}$
$7^1/_2$	7.5	56.25	+	81.	11.72	$11^{23}/_{32}$
$7^9/_{16}$	7.5625	57.19	+	81.	11.76	$11^3/_4$
$7^5/_8$	7.625	58.14	+	81.	11.80	$11^{25}/_{32}$
$7^{11}/_{16}$	7.6875	59.1	+	81.	11.84	$11^{27}/_{32}$
$7^3/_4$	7.75	60.06	+	81.	11.88	$11^7/_8$
$7^{13}/_{16}$	7.8125	61.04	+	81.	11.92	$11^{29}/_{32}$
$7^7/_8$	7.875	62.02	+	81.	11.96	$11^{31}/_{32}$
$7^{15}/_{16}$	7.9375	63.	+	81.	12.00	12
8	8	64.	+	81.	12.04	$12^1/_{32}$

STAIR STRINGER HYPOTENUSE TABLE FOR A 9⅛" UNIT RUN: $a^2 + b^2 = c^2$.

Rise in fractions (a)	Rise in decimals (a)	Square of the rise (a^2)		Square of the run (b^2)	Unit hypotenuse (c) Decimals	Fractions
7	7	49.	+	83.27	11.50	11½
7 1/16	7.0625	49.88	+	83.27	11.54	11 17/32
7 1/8	7.125	50.77	+	83.27	11.58	11 9/16
7 3/16	7.1875	51.66	+	83.27	11.62	11 5/8
7 1/4	7.25	52.56	+	83.27	11.65	11 21/32
7 5/16	7.3125	53.47	+	83.27	11.69	11 11/16
7 3/8	7.375	54.39	+	83.27	11.73	11 23/32
7 7/16	7.4375	55.32	+	83.27	11.77	11 25/32
7 1/2	7.5	56.25	+	83.27	11.81	11 13/16
7 9/16	7.5625	57.19	+	83.27	11.85	11 27/32
7 5/8	7.625	58.14	+	83.27	11.89	11 7/8
7 11/16	7.6875	59.1	+	83.27	11.93	11 15/16
7 3/4	7.75	60.06	+	83.27	11.97	11 31/32
7 13/16	7.8125	61.04	+	83.27	12.01	12
7 7/8	7.875	62.02	+	83.27	12.05	12 1/16
7 15/16	7.9375	63.	+	83.27	12.09	12 3/32
8	8	64.	+	83.27	12.14	12 1/8

STAIR STRINGER HYPOTENUSE TABLE FOR A 9¼" UNIT RUN: $a^2 + b^2 = c^2$.

Rise in fractions (a)	Rise in decimals (a)	Square of the rise (a^2)		Square of the run (b^2)	Unit hypotenuse (c) Decimals	Fractions
7	7	49.	+	85.56	11.60	11 19/32
7 1/16	7.0625	49.88	+	85.56	11.64	11 5/8
7 1/8	7.125	50.77	+	85.56	11.68	11 11/16
7 3/16	7.1875	51.66	+	85.56	11.71	11 23/32
7 1/4	7.25	52.56	+	85.56	11.75	11 3/4
7 5/16	7.3125	53.47	+	85.56	11.79	11 25/32
7 3/8	7.375	54.39	+	85.56	11.83	11 13/16
7 7/16	7.4375	55.32	+	85.56	11.87	11 7/8
7 1/2	7.5	56.25	+	85.56	11.91	11 29/32
7 9/16	7.5625	57.19	+	85.56	11.95	11 15/16
7 5/8	7.625	58.14	+	85.56	11.99	12
7 11/16	7.6875	59.1	+	85.56	12.03	12 1/32
7 3/4	7.75	60.06	+	85.56	12.07	12 1/16
7 13/16	7.8125	61.04	+	85.56	12.11	12 3/32
7 7/8	7.875	62.02	+	85.56	12.15	12 5/32
7 15/16	7.9375	63.	+	85.56	12.19	12 3/16
8	8	64.	+	85.56	12.23	12 7/32

STAIR STRINGER HYPOTENUSE TABLE FOR A $9\tfrac{3}{8}''$ UNIT RUN: $a^2 + b^2 = c^2$.

Rise in fractions (a)	Rise in decimals (a)	Square of the rise (a^2)		Square of the run (b^2)	Unit hypotenuse (c)	
					Decimals	Fractions
7	7	49.	+	87.89	11.70	$11\tfrac{11}{16}$
$7\tfrac{1}{16}$	7.0625	49.88	+	87.89	11.74	$11\tfrac{3}{4}$
$7\tfrac{1}{8}$	7.125	50.77	+	87.89	11.78	$11\tfrac{25}{32}$
$7\tfrac{3}{16}$	7.1875	51.66	+	87.89	11.81	$11\tfrac{13}{16}$
$7\tfrac{1}{4}$	7.25	52.56	+	87.89	11.85	$11\tfrac{27}{32}$
$7\tfrac{5}{16}$	7.3125	53.47	+	87.89	11.89	$11\tfrac{7}{8}$
$7\tfrac{3}{8}$	7.375	54.39	+	87.89	11.93	$11\tfrac{15}{16}$
$7\tfrac{7}{16}$	7.4375	55.32	+	87.89	11.97	$11\tfrac{31}{32}$
$7\tfrac{1}{2}$	7.5	56.25	+	87.89	12.01	12
$7\tfrac{9}{16}$	7.5625	57.19	+	87.89	12.05	$12\tfrac{1}{32}$
$7\tfrac{5}{8}$	7.625	58.14	+	87.89	12.08	$12\tfrac{3}{32}$
$7\tfrac{11}{16}$	7.6875	59.1	+	87.89	12.12	$12\tfrac{1}{8}$
$7\tfrac{3}{4}$	7.75	60.06	+	87.89	12.16	$12\tfrac{5}{32}$
$7\tfrac{13}{16}$	7.8125	61.04	+	87.89	12.20	$12\tfrac{3}{16}$
$7\tfrac{7}{8}$	7.875	62.02	+	87.89	12.24	$12\tfrac{1}{4}$
$7\tfrac{15}{16}$	7.9375	63.	+	87.89	12.28	$12\tfrac{9}{32}$
8	8	64.	+	87.89	12.32	$12\tfrac{5}{16}$

STAIR STRINGER HYPOTENUSE TABLE FOR A $9\tfrac{1}{2}''$ UNIT RUN: $a^2 + b^2 = c^2$.

Rise in fractions (a)	Rise in decimals (a)	Square of the rise (a^2)		Square of the run (b^2)	Unit hypotenuse (c)	
					Decimals	Fractions
7	7	49.	+	90.25	11.80	$11\tfrac{13}{16}$
$7\tfrac{1}{16}$	7.0625	49.88	+	90.25	11.84	$11\tfrac{27}{32}$
$7\tfrac{1}{8}$	7.125	50.77	+	90.25	11.87	$11\tfrac{7}{8}$
$7\tfrac{3}{16}$	7.1875	51.66	+	90.25	11.91	$11\tfrac{29}{32}$
$7\tfrac{1}{4}$	7.25	52.56	+	90.25	11.95	$11\tfrac{15}{16}$
$7\tfrac{5}{16}$	7.3125	53.47	+	90.25	11.99	12
$7\tfrac{3}{8}$	7.375	54.39	+	90.25	12.03	$12\tfrac{1}{32}$
$7\tfrac{7}{16}$	7.4375	55.32	+	90.25	12.07	$12\tfrac{1}{16}$
$7\tfrac{1}{2}$	7.5	56.25	+	90.25	12.10	$12\tfrac{3}{32}$
$7\tfrac{9}{16}$	7.5625	57.19	+	90.25	12.14	$12\tfrac{1}{8}$
$7\tfrac{5}{8}$	7.625	58.14	+	90.25	12.18	$12\tfrac{3}{16}$
$7\tfrac{11}{16}$	7.6875	59.1	+	90.25	12.22	$12\tfrac{7}{32}$
$7\tfrac{3}{4}$	7.75	60.06	+	90.25	12.26	$12\tfrac{1}{4}$
$7\tfrac{13}{16}$	7.8125	61.04	+	90.25	12.30	$12\tfrac{9}{32}$
$7\tfrac{7}{8}$	7.875	62.02	+	90.25	12.34	$12\tfrac{11}{32}$
$7\tfrac{15}{16}$	7.9375	63.	+	90.25	12.38	$12\tfrac{3}{8}$
8	8	64.	+	90.25	12.42	$12\tfrac{13}{32}$

STAIR STRINGER HYPOTENUSE TABLE FOR A 9⅝" UNIT: $a^2 + b^2 = c^2$.

Rise in fractions (a)	Rise in decimals (a)	Square of the rise (a^2)		Square of the run (b^2)	Unit hypotenuse (c) Decimals	Fractions
7	7	49.	+	92.64	11.90	11²⁹/₃₂
7¹/₁₆	7.0625	49.88	+	92.64	11.94	11¹⁵/₁₆
7¹/₈	7.125	50.77	+	92.64	11.98	11³¹/₃₂
7³/₁₆	7.1875	51.66	+	92.64	12.01	12
7¹/₄	7.25	52.56	+	92.64	12.05	12¹/₁₆
7⁵/₁₆	7.3125	53.47	+	92.64	12.09	12³/₃₂
7³/₈	7.375	54.39	+	92.64	12.13	12¹/₈
7⁷/₁₆	7.4375	55.32	+	92.64	12.16	12⁵/₃₂
7¹/₂	7.5	56.25	+	92.64	12.20	12³/₁₆
7⁹/₁₆	7.5625	57.19	+	92.64	12.24	12¹/₄
7⁵/₈	7.625	58.14	+	92.64	12.28	12⁹/₃₂
7¹¹/₁₆	7.6875	59.1	+	92.64	12.32	12⁵/₁₆
7³/₄	7.75	60.06	+	92.64	12.36	12¹¹/₃₂
7¹³/₁₆	7.8125	61.04	+	92.64	12.40	12¹³/₃₂
7⁷/₈	7.875	62.02	+	92.64	12.44	12⁷/₁₆
7¹⁵/₁₆	7.9375	63.	+	92.64	12.48	12¹⁵/₃₂
8	8	64.	+	92.64	12.52	12¹/₂

STAIR STRINGER HYPOTENUSE TABLE FOR A 9¾" UNIT RUN: $a^2 + b^2 = c^2$.

Rise in fractions (a)	Rise in decimals (a)	Square of the rise (a^2)		Square of the run (b^2)	Unit hypotenuse (c) Decimals	Fractions
7	7	49.	+	95.06	12.	12
7¹/₁₆	7.0625	49.88	+	95.06	12.04	12¹/₃₂
7¹/₈	7.125	50.77	+	95.06	12.08	12¹/₁₆
7³/₁₆	7.1875	51.66	+	95.06	12.11	12¹/₈
7¹/₄	7.25	52.56	+	95.06	12.15	12⁵/₃₂
7⁵/₁₆	7.3125	53.47	+	95.06	12.19	12³/₁₆
7³/₈	7.375	54.39	+	95.06	12.23	12⁷/₃₂
7⁷/₁₆	7.4375	55.32	+	95.06	12.26	12¹/₄
7¹/₂	7.5	56.25	+	95.06	12.30	12⁵/₁₆
7⁹/₁₆	7.5625	57.19	+	95.06	12.34	12¹¹/₃₂
7⁵/₈	7.625	58.14	+	95.06	12.38	12³/₈
7¹¹/₁₆	7.6875	59.1	+	95.06	12.42	12¹³/₃₂
7³/₄	7.75	60.06	+	95.06	12.45	12⁷/₁₆
7¹³/₁₆	7.8125	61.04	+	95.06	12.49	12¹/₂
7⁷/₈	7.875	62.02	+	95.06	12.53	12¹⁷/₃₂
7¹⁵/₁₆	7.9375	63.	+	95.06	12.57	12⁹/₁₆
8	8	64.	+	95.06	12.61	12¹⁹/₃₂

STAIR STRINGER HYPOTENUSE TABLE FOR A 9 7/8″ UNIT RUN: $a^2 + b^2 = c^2$.

Rise in fractions (a)	Rise in decimals (a)	Square of the rise (a^2)		Square of the run (b^2)	Unit hypotenuse (c) Decimals	Fractions
7	7	49.	+	97.52	12.10	12 3/32
7 1/16	7.0625	49.88	+	97.52	12.14	12 1/8
7 1/8	7.125	50.77	+	97.52	12.18	12 3/16
7 3/16	7.1875	51.66	+	97.52	12.21	12 7/32
7 1/4	7.25	52.56	+	97.52	12.25	12 1/4
7 5/16	7.3125	53.47	+	97.52	12.29	12 9/32
7 3/8	7.375	54.39	+	97.52	12.33	12 5/16
7 7/16	7.4375	55.32	+	97.52	12.36	12 3/8
7 1/2	7.5	56.25	+	97.52	12.40	12 13/32
7 9/16	7.5625	57.19	+	97.52	12.44	17 7/16
7 5/8	7.625	58.14	+	97.52	12.48	12 15/32
7 11/16	7.6875	59.1	+	97.52	12.51	12 1/2
7 3/4	7.75	60.06	+	97.52	12.55	12 9/16
7 13/16	7.8125	61.04	+	97.52	12.59	12 19/32
7 7/8	7.875	62.02	+	97.52	12.63	12 5/8
7 15/16	7.9375	63.	+	97.52	12.67	12 21/32
8	8	64.	+	97.52	12.71	12 23/32

STAIR STRINGER HYPOTENUSE TABLE FOR A 10″ UNIT RUN: $a^2 + b^2 = c^2$.

Rise in fractions (a)	Rise in decimals (a)	Square of the rise (a^2)		Square of the run (b^2)	Unit hypotenuse (c) Decimals	Fractions
7	7	49.	+	100	12.21	12 7/32
7 1/16	7.0625	49.88	+	100	12.24	12 1/4
7 1/8	7.125	50.77	+	100	12.28	12 9/32
7 3/16	7.1875	51.66	+	100	12.32	12 5/16
7 1/4	7.25	52.56	+	100	12.35	12 11/32
7 5/16	7.3125	53.47	+	100	12.39	12 3/8
7 3/8	7.375	54.39	+	100	12.43	12 7/16
7 7/16	7.4375	55.32	+	100	12.46	12 15/32
7 1/2	7.5	56.25	+	100	12.50	12 1/2
7 9/16	7.5625	57.19	+	100	12.54	12 17/32
7 5/8	7.625	58.14	+	100	12.58	12 9/16
7 11/16	7.6875	59.1	+	100	12.61	12 5/8
7 3/4	7.75	60.06	+	100	12.65	12 21/32
7 13/16	7.8125	61.04	+	100	12.69	12 11/16
7 7/8	7.875	62.02	+	100	12.73	12 23/32
7 15/16	7.9375	63.	+	100	12.77	12 3/4
8	8	64.	+	100	12.81	12 13/16

Index